PETER DAY lives on the banks of the Milwaukee River with his wife Lorraine and their two children. As editor of *The Living Church,* an outstanding weekly magazine reporting the news, the work, and the thought of the Episcopal Church, he is well-known in Church and literary circles. He also contributes a sparkling and widely read weekly column in *The Living Church,* "Sorts and Conditions."

Young Peter was educated in public schools, at St. John's Military Academy, Delafield, Wisconsin, and at Dartmouth College. His early years of life in the rectory (his father was an Episcopal clergyman) pointed the way to his career. Upon graduation from Dartmouth he joined the staff of *The Living Church,* a month later became managing editor, and in 1952 took up his present position of editor.

Among the many areas of Church life that Mr. Day has served are Christian education, welfare, social relations, and citizenship. He also served for two years as president of The Associated Church Press, and is an acolyte in his home parish in Whitefish Bay, Wisconsin. He has been the president of three community-chest-supported social agencies in the Milwaukee area.

His interests seem to be all-embracing—family, church, community, recreation, literature — and he claims to have two versions of The Great American novel in his attic. But writing *Saints on Main Street,* meeting weekly deadlines, and publishing *The Living Church,* have so far prevented him from completing them.

SAINTS ON MAIN STREET

The Gospel for the Ordinary Christian

* * BY PETER DAY * *

GREENWICH · CONNECTICUT · 1960

LIBRARY OF CONGRESS CATALOG CARD NUMBER: 60-5360
PRINTED IN THE UNITED STATES OF AMERICA
311-1259-C-5

Preface

IF YOU ARE a member of the Christian Church you are a saint. This was the view of the New Testament writers who addressed their letters to the "saints" in Greece and Asia, and concluded with greetings from the "saints" with whom they were staying.

In these same letters, there are many examples of the fact that saints are not always as good as they ought to be. Some of them were boisterous and unruly. Some of them ate and drank too much. Some of them got mixed up with strange doctrines that came in for apostolic condemnation. Yet they were saints. They were people set apart from the general run of humanity, having a special relation to God.

Today, the word "saint" is ordinarily used only for Christians who do a better than average job of being saints. There is, however, a world-wide renewal of interest in the implications of the Gospel for the ordinary lives of ordinary church people. If we are indeed saints, if we do have a special relationship to God, what are the results of this relationship as we go about our daily tasks in home and office and factory, and in political and social life? How do the saints on Main Street or Broadway or Rural Route #2 differ from their neighbors who know nothing about Christ? What is their ministry as Christian laymen and women?

This renewal of interest in the ministry of the laity is paralleled by a general rediscovery of the relevance of the New Testament to the predicament of twentieth-century man. The Bible's suggestions about what to do while you are waiting for the end of the world have a fresh and contemporary ring to a generation that is waiting for somebody to make the final mistake in international affairs.

In thinking of the role of the Christian layman in the world, we are tempted to graft a Christian theology onto a secular ideology. Our ideas about God and grace and salvation are put to work in the service of concepts about men and parishes and nations and civilization that have very little relation to Christianity.

A sound Christian ideology, however, begins with the Christian insight that we are indeed living in "these last days"—that the ultimate issues of death and judgment, of heaven and hell, have become practical and immediate concerns for everybody. This book attempts to provide a framework for an "ideology of the laity" based upon the Bible and the Book of Common Prayer. The Prayer Book collects have become so familiar to us that we often pay little attention to the plain and obvious meaning of their words. They are used here, without interpretation or explanation, as a way of summing up in prayer the ideas that have been discussed in the immediately preceding section.

It is the belief of the writer of this book that the next great breakthrough of the Gospel upon the life of the ordinary parish of the Episcopal Church will be in the field of Christian social relations, by way of a new and deeper understanding of what the ministry of the laity is and means. The same renewed understanding may, in other Christian communions, be finding quite different forms of expression. In Roman Catholicism, it is an effort to bring the Church back to the people, both in worship and in new and daring experiments in evangelism among the working classes. In some Protestant denominations, the same ecumenical discovery of the shape of the Christian fellowship may result in a heightened understanding of Baptism and Holy Communion, a revived liturgical sense, a higher appreciation of the place of the ordained ministry.

All of us are learning from each other, because all of us are facing the fact that the Church of Christ is not the good people of the community called together for prayer, but something sharply marked off from the secular community, with a different origin and a different goal—a fellowship of saints.

Anglicans, Roman Catholics, and Protestants are writing, thinking, and working independently toward remarkably similar results, and reports from Germany, Belgium, France, England, Asia, and Africa indicate that the entire Christian world is involved in a common discovery comparable to the way in which scientific discoveries are sometimes made independently by several researchers at the same time.

What this common discovery means in the life of the Episcopal Church may serve as an illustration of the fact that moving toward a common goal requires movement in different directions from different starting-points. What one Church needs to accomplish may be something that another Church has already achieved. Yet, theorizing about the ministry of the laity means little unless it is brought to bear on the existential situation of existing Churches. And this involves assessing the impact of the Gospel upon the specific ethos and structure and goals of each.

Accordingly, what is happening to parishes of the Episcopal Church is significant not only to Episcopalians themselves but to all who are engaged in the common task of proclaiming the Gospel in today's world.

The Department of Christian Social Relations of the Episcopal Church, through its Division of Christian Citizenship under the leadership of the Rev. Arthur Walmsley, is in the thick of this process of discovery; and he as well as his predecessor, the Rev. M. Moran Weston, and the director of the Department, the Rev. Almon R. Pepper, with fellow-workers too numerous to mention, have had much to do with the development of my ideas in this area. To the extent that the book is intelligible and logical, the credit belongs to my wife, Lorraine, a most exacting editorial adviser. And if you read these words in print, it will be because Jean Drysdale reduced a tattered and much-interpolated manuscript to such shape that a publisher could make sense of it.

PETER DAY

Contents

For the Son of man is as a man, taking a far journey, who left his house, and gave authority to his servants, and to every man his work. . . . St. Mark 13:34

* * 1 * *

Rediscovering the Laity

CLERICALISM, the tendency to turn all important functions in religion over to the clergy, seems to be one of the most stubborn problems of church life. One form of it, as exemplified by Roman Catholicism, consists of magnifying the governmental authority and spiritual powers of the priestly hierarchy to the point where the laity are merely the passive recipients of a gospel, a sacramental system, and a body of church law dispensed by the clergy.

This distortion of the shape of the Christian Church is rightly condemned by members of other churches. But, in another form, the disease of clericalism is just as common in churches at the opposite end of the ecclesiastical scale. A church service that consists of a monologue by the minister; a no-smoking, no-drinking, no-dancing, no-cardplaying ethical code which only ministers are expected to keep—these are the marks of another kind of clericalism which, like the authoritarian Roman form, seems to be based upon the assumption that the laity know little and care even less about the things of God.

But clericalism is not a disease of the clergy; it is a disease of the whole Church, clergy and laity alike. Its root cause is the failure of the laity to fulfill their role in the life of the Church.

Under ideal conditions, there would be differences between clerical and lay function in the Church, but there would be no real conflict between the two kinds of ministry. As St. Paul said, writing to the Corinthians, "There are varieties of gifts, but the same Spirit; and there are varieties of service, but the same Lord; and there are varieties of working but it is the same God who inspires them all in everyone."

Throughout Christendom today, there appears to be a stirring among clergy and laity alike toward a renewed awareness of the importance of the ministry of the laity. It is the purpose of this book to reflect some of the light of this renewed awareness upon the ordinary layman's concept of himself as a Christian, a churchman, a parent, a citizen, an economic producer and consumer, and a member of the human race, in a time of global crisis.

The phrase, "the ministry of the laity," has, for modern ears, a clerical ring. It suggests, somehow, that the layman should achieve recognition as a kind of junior minister. This is not what is meant by those who are actively writing, thinking, and exploring in this field.

For example, a layman of the Episcopal Church who becomes a lay reader and then becomes interested in the perpetual diaconate, finally going on into the priesthood, is not necessarily carrying the ministry of the laity by logical steps to its fulfillment in the ranks of the ordained clergy. This may be a very worthwhile and necessary course of spiritual development for a particular individual. But some of us, presumably the vast majority, must expect to find our course of spiritual development in other directions. The vocation of being a layman is neither lower nor easier than the clerical vocation. It is a different calling, embodying the gifts of the same Spirit, the service of the same Lord, and the workings of the same God.

In the Bible, all Christians are "ministers," but not all are apostles, elders, prophets, or pastors. Some Christian communions, with a vivid recollection of the evils of medieval clericalism, avoid using the term "clergy" for their ordained ministry. But the result often appears to be that a biblical word referring to everybody's Christian vocation has been pre-empted for the more specialized, professional vocation of leading the worship of the Christian fellowship. Very early in Church history, those who had this special professional ministry received the designation of "cleric" in recognition of the fact that they had cast their lot (Greek, *kleros*) with the Church. And in most of Protestantism today, no matter what terminology may be used, the minister faces the special duties, privileges, and temptations that go with his specialized status in the life of the congregation.

Amateurs in religion are needed as well as professionals. In sports, an amateur is a person who plays the game for the love of it; a professional is a person who does the same thing for a living. This simple distinction between amateur and professional, however, doesn't work out very well even in sports. Big-time amateurs are often hard to distinguish from pros in the matter of making a living out of their efforts. And only a man who really loves football, baseball, tennis, or golf will get anywhere in professional competition.

The clergyman is, generally speaking, a man who gets his living from the Church. The layman makes his living in some other way and therefore remains an "amateur," although in church life as in some sports the distinction is blurred by exceptions, anomalies, and borderline cases. Still, it is true that a clergyman is a person who not only loves God and His Church but has decided to make a lifework out of this love.

More than 99% of the religion that is or can be practiced in this world must be on an amateur basis, for obvious economic reasons. However, religion is not a sport or a hobby. It is a life-and-death matter, involving the destiny of men and nations. It is easy to understand why the "professionals"—the clergy—are likely to suffer acute anxiety when they see an amateur juggling priceless theological ideas and church principles as casually as if they were kitchen china.

Yet if the ministry of the laity is ever to have a broader meaning than an ever higher level of "church work" culminating in a sort of graduation into the professional ministry for the star layman, theology must have a new impact upon the laity, and the laity must have a new impact on theology. G. K. Chesterton's famous remark, "Whatever is worth doing is worth doing badly," is very much to the point here. The work of knowing Christ and making Him known needs doing far more than it needs to be done well. The joy and spiritual growth that come even from the unskilled exercise of Christian faith are a part of that abundant life which Christ promised to His followers.

Almighty God, who hast given thine only Son to be unto us both a sacrifice for sin, and also an ensample of godly life; Give us grace that we may always most thankfully receive that his inestimable benefit, and also daily endeavour ourselves to follow the blessed steps of his most holy life; through the same thy Son Jesus Christ our Lord. Amen.

Book of Common Prayer, page 171

One example of a place where the amateur's role cannot be filled by the professional is in the care of the most valuable and complex mechanism of today's world—babies. A generation ago, it seemed that the doctors, psychologists, and other assorted experts were about to declare parents unnecessary. But, in institutions where babies were cared for under sterile and orderly conditions that would prevent their developing either diseases or complexes, they failed to gain, many sickened, and some unaccountably died.

Under unskilled parental handling, a baby turns out to be a very tough and resilient creature who can survive many loving mistakes. A similar inner logic applies to Christianity. The thing that causes Christianity to sicken and stop growing in the family or the parish or the individual soul is the same thing that causes babies to pine away under theoretically ideal hospital conditions—lack of loving, lack of personal contact, lack of amateur attention.

Doctors and institutional executives cannot do all of the loving that babies need, and the priest cannot do all the loving that his community requires. However, the analogy between cleric and medic must not be pressed too far. The place of the clergyman in the life of the Church is not just a matter of his full-time dedication to his ministerial task, his long years of training, and his appointment by duly constituted authority. These are the things that make him a professional, but he is more than a professional.

Since the ministry of the laity is a part of a whole in which the ministry of the clergy is vitally important, we need to understand both kinds of ministry in order to understand either one fully. The nature of both is based on the nature of the Church itself.

The Church is, as described by St. Paul, the "body of Christ." Jesus, in the Gospel According to St. John, uses a similar biological metaphor when He says, "I am the vine and ye are the branches." The Church is an organism. The physical and material constituents of that organism are, like the cells and tissues of a body, the vehicle of a life.

As natural science has gone forward in the past few centuries, the mysteries of living organisms have become even more wonderful than they were when St. Paul wrote his epistles. We know now that a man can eat eggs, meat, and vegetables and incorporate them into his living tissues; and yet that if he has lost a kidney, he cannot replace it with one from an animal or even another man. Only a kidney from his identical twin can be transplanted into his body successfully. A body has its own principles of organization and will not tolerate the intrusion of something very similar, but differing minutely in structure.

In the body that is the Church, certain of the human "cells" are set apart, as in a biological organism, for certain functions. The details of these functions may vary widely at different times in the body's history. The communions which have retained the historic episcopate are more concerned to maintain this biological continuity in the ministry than to preserve the functions which were anciently attached to a particular order. Ministries of Reformation origin tend toward an opposite emphasis. For example, the duties of a deacon in the Episcopal Church do not correspond to the ancient duties of deacons nearly as much as those of deacons in many Protestant Churches. Protestants are quite right in saying that bishops and presbyters in the New Testament were more like each other than either is like his twentieth-century counterpart in Roman Catholicism or Anglicanism. But it is also true that, while there is a time in the life of a tadpole when he is more like a fish than a frog, he is a frog and not a fish, all the same.

The epistle to St. Timothy speaks of a "gift" (Greek, *charisma*) that is in Timothy because of the Church's ordaining act. This special *charisma* of ordination does not give the minister an inside track to heaven, nor does it make him automatically better or wiser than other men. But it does make him God's representative to His people, for better or for worse—the man whose preaching is the Church's preaching, whose offering of the Holy Communion is the Church's offering, whose blessing and absolution are the Church's blessing and absolution.

The Book of Common Prayer provides for differentiating, or setting apart, the Church's bishops, priests, and deacons by the laying on of hands with prayer in a sacramental rite which makes them different from what they were before. In this act, the Church, the body of Christ, gives them a *charisma*, a gift, a special endowment of the Holy Spirit, as Christ gave such a special endowment to His apostles. The performance of this act in the life of the Church is one of the functions of the bishops. The Episcopal Church is called "episcopal" because of its insistence that nobody but a bishop has Christ's authority to ordain new bishops, priests, and deacons in His Church. How to reconcile this once universally accepted principle of the Church's "biology" with the congregational and presbyterial forms of the ministry is one of the big problems of Church unity. However, there is real hope that the growing understanding of the ministry of the laity will provide both sides of the Church unity argument with higher and better ground for their encounter in ecumenical debate. The Catholic communions are learning that the status of layman is an important and dignified "order" in the Church with its own responsibilities, powers, and duties. The non-episcopal communions are learning that there is a difference between clerical and lay ministry and that the place of the laity is not made more important and dignified by the obliteration of that difference.

The relation of the ministry to the people of the Church has varied widely from time to time and place to place. It is influenced by the cultural conditions in which it is set, and by conditions within the Church. In the medieval period, when the average churchman could neither read nor write, the clergy were authorities on everything—on all kinds of knowledge, on the rights and privileges of individuals and groups, as well as on matters of theology and the conduct of church affairs. Even in the present day, the relation of clergy to people is not the same in different communions nor even in different settings within one communion. Any generalization about what is inherently a clergyman's function and what is inherently a layman's function must necessarily be taken with a grain of salt.

Yet, a reasonably clear distinction between clergyman and layman goes back to the very earliest days of the Church when the believers "continued steadfastly in the apostles' doctrine and fellowship, and in the breaking of bread, and in the prayers." It is plain, not just from this one text, but from the description of apostolic leadership and authority throughout the Book of Acts, that the "doctrine" and the "fellowship" of the Church were under the apostles' control. "The breaking of bread" and "the prayers" similarly represented the body of church worship instituted by Christ and taught by the apostles.

But the Church does not exist only in the realm of ideas. It is a living organism, a biological phenomenon, the "body of Christ." As such, it has a genetic identity conveyed from generation to generation, not by its broad membership, but by its "chromosomes" and "genes." These could not exist apart from the general membership, but within it they have a unique and normative role in shaping the entire body along the lines originally laid down by Christ.

Hence, a proper concept of the ministry of the laity involves recognizing that the ministry of the clergy has special functions which the laity should not try to supplant. The norms for the Church's doctrine and fellowship are provided primarily by the clergy rather than by the laity. The application of these apostolic norms to daily living is the Christian ministry for which the layman is primarily responsible.

O Almighty God, who hast built thy Church upon the foundation of the Apostles and Prophets, Jesus Christ himself being the head corner-stone; Grant us so to be joined together in unity of spirit by their doctrine, that we may be made an holy temple acceptable unto thee; through the same Jesus Christ our Lord. Amen.

Book of Common Prayer, page 254

* * * * *

Theology is a descriptive science. It describes something that existed before it was described by theologians. The Church existed before St. Paul described it as the body of Christ, and the ministry existed before anybody tried to explain what it was or how it worked. In most things, the Church first "did what came naturally," and explained afterwards what it was doing.

Accordingly, the relationships between clergy and laity described in the New Testament represent, not the carrying out of an apostolic "theory of the ministry," but the working out of the fact of the ministry as the Church grew and developed in the first-century world.

People who asked St. Peter what he was doing in those first days after Pentecost were given a ready answer. He and his fellow-disciples were telling some good news which everybody needed to know about.

Though the people of Israel had rejected their King when He came to them in peace and lowliness, though their rulers had conspired against Him and killed Him, God had raised Him from the dead and He would soon return in glory to usher in a new order of things.

"In the last days," said St. Peter, quoting the prophet Joel, "it shall be, God declares, that I will pour out my spirit upon all flesh, and your sons and your daughters shall prophesy, and your young men shall see visions, and your old men shall dream dreams. . . . And it shall be that whoever calls on the name of the Lord shall be saved."

Those who wished to have a part in this new order should turn away from their sins, be baptized (washed) in the name of Jesus, and believe in the good news that Jesus was their Lord and Saviour.

Coming events cast their shadows before. The healing of the sick, the feeding of the hungry, the clothing of the naked, the liberation of prisoners in the wake of the proclamation of the good news—these were harbingers of the new day, as the rising sun catches a cloud or a treetop before it peeps over the horizon.

Most particularly, within the Christian fellowship the presence of the Lord who was soon to be revealed to all the world was made known in the breaking of the bread and the partaking of the cup of the New Covenant that had been established in His blood. As baptism was the act of entry into the fellowship of those who were to be the Israel of the future, so their breaking of bread together was an act of communion—common life—with Him in anticipation of the new age.

When the infant Church first appeared on the

scene, it had a ready-made ministry. There were twelve —according to the number of the ancient twelve tribes of Israel—who had been with Jesus through His earthly ministry and had special authority from Him to speak and act in His name. The Church gathered itself around them and called them "apostles"—men who had been sent. They were authoritative witnesses to what had happened, they were the ones to settle disputes, and if anybody failed to live up to the community's standards of behavior, the apostles were the ones to decide whether such a person should be thrown out.

It was not long before dozens of reasons led to a passing on of some measure of the apostles' authority to other Christians. St. Luke gives indications of some of the reasons in Chapters 6, 7, and 8 of the Book of Acts. The Greek-speaking Christians wanted to have something to say in the matter of taking care of the community's needy. Some of these men were notably fervent in their life and powerful in their witness. The whole enterprise was getting too big for the apostles' personal attention.

So seven subsidiary ministers were appointed. Although the Book of Acts does not say so, they are traditionally regarded as the first deacons. The people chose them, the apostles approved them, and set them apart for their ministry with prayer and the laying on of hands. The seven didn't confine themselves to passing out relief to the widows. They preached, baptized, worked miracles.

However, even so powerful an evangelist as Philip was subject to apostolic authority. His highly successful ministry in Samaria (where the Gospel was brought for the first time to a non-Jewish community) was not complete until the apostles came down, approved what they saw, and laid their hands on the Samaritans' heads.

The point of this story in Acts 8 may be that only the apostles could give the gift of the Holy Ghost. It may be that the extension of membership in the new Israel to Samaritans (and ultimately to Gentiles) was reserved for the apostles. In either case, it is an example of the fact that from the very start the Church possessed a central authority, to which the Holy Ghost Himself bore witness, for ordering its life and affairs. There was much give and take between this central authority and the general membership. People could argue with the apostles and tell them they were wrong. Nevertheless, the apostles' decisions settled things.

Today, if the Episcopal Church says that only the priest may celebrate Holy Communion, it does so in the broader context of regarding the priest as deriving the general authority for his ministry from the apostles. Under the direction of the bishop (who in turn is under the direction of his brother bishops), the priest gives or withholds absolution and blessing as Christ's agent. As the Holy Ghost bore witness of the apostles' authority to St. Philip's Samaritan converts, so the Church believes the Holy Ghost today bears witness to the authority of the apostolic ministry of the bishops, priests, and deacons, each in its proper context and with the functions appropriate to our own times.

So a layman is not a priest or an ordained minister. He is not in charge of the congregation, nor is the whole body of laypeople able to carry on their Church life in the absence of, or in opposition to, their clergy.

By reserving to the priest the office of celebrant at the Holy Communion the Episcopal Church bears witness to his authority as president of the vestry, as authoritative preacher of the Gospel, as guide of the women's guilds, as chief teacher of the Sunday school, as the executive head of each aspect of the parish's life. He is the head of the parish family. He is Christ's representative in the parish. As such, his authority is the authority of love, of self-sacrifice, of everything that we associate with the name of Christ or the idea of a father.

O Lord Jesus Christ, who at thy first coming didst send thy messenger to prepare thy way before thee; Grant that the ministers and stewards of thy mysteries may likewise so prepare and make ready thy way, by turning the hearts of the disobedient to the wisdom of the just, that at thy second coming to judge the world we may be found an acceptable people in thy sight, who livest and reignest with the Father and the Holy Spirit ever, one God, world without end. Amen.

Book of Common Prayer, page 93

If all Christian pastors were paragons of wisdom and virtue, fitted in all ways to be Christ's representatives on earth, no more would need to be said. But since they are only men, and sinners like ourselves, their exercise of the authority of Christ is subject to checks and balances. The laity, too, are saints. They are the body of Christ, bearers of His life, and witnesses to His Gospel. The picture of the Church given in the New Testament shows the laity participating in church government in many ways. They helped in the selection of Matthias to replace Judas as one of the twelve apostles. They chose the men whom the apostles ordained deacons. "The apostles and the elders, *with the whole Church*," took part in the Council of Jerusalem which made the big decision about admitting Gentiles to Christianity without requiring them to embrace Judaism first.

Moreover, when the New Testament uses the word "Church" the emphasis is distinctly on the laity. For the Greek word *ekklesia* which the New Testament writers used was roughly equivalent to our modern expression "town meeting."

The town officers by themselves do not constitute the town meeting. Nor is the meeting duly assembled for business unless its proper officers are present in their proper roles. Similarly, the Church as the assembly of the people of God is not just a gathering of Christian people, nor is it just a clerical conclave; it is one body, with both clerical and lay members, each of whom has his own "liturgy" (public duty) to perform.

Somehow, over the course of history, the place of the clergy has become more and more prominent in the life of the Church and the place of the laity less and less prominent. Perhaps the laity defaulted in their "liturgy" first, leaving the clergy no alternative but to move in and take over. Perhaps the clergy made church life more and more a matter for professionals and less and less a matter for amateurs. Whatever the reason, the fact is that throughout Christianity today, from Romanism at one extreme to Congregationalism at the other, the priest or minister is not merely the leader of the church's life of worship, thought, and action—he is practically the whole show.

As soon as an abuse is identified, it is on its way to correction. In nearly every Christian communion, note-worthy efforts are being made to restore the laity to their place of being active, rather than merely passive, Chris-tians. The first thing the active Christian does is to wor-ship God—this is his supreme activity, and both the starting point and the goal of his other activities. And virtually all Christendom is busy rediscovering the fact that the worship of the Church is an activity in which both the officiant and the congregation have an active part to play.

Roman Catholics are trying to put as much of the service as possible into the language of the people, and to get the people to make the responses that have been provided for them from time immemorial. Presbyterians, Methodists, Baptists, are turning away from the long monologue prayer and the long sermon to a more dy-namic kind of service with enhanced congregational par-ticipation. The Episcopalian may congratulate himself that both his Roman and his Protestant brothers are modifying their public worship along the lines of the Book of Common Prayer.

It is true that the worship of the Prayer Book is less in need of radical reform than the worship of most other communions. But rewriting the forms of worship will not solve all problems; and it is remarkable how passive the laity of the Episcopal Church can be about their Christianity and how contented the clergy of the Epis-copal Church can be with their people's passiveness.

Though it is hard to be a mere spectator at the Prayer

Book services of Morning Prayer and Holy Communion, many thousands of Episcopalians have learned the trick. And other thousands have learned to make all the responses, to stand, sit, and kneel, to find their places in the book, etc., and yet have not learned to carry the activity of their worship into their daily living.

The problem confronting all Christian Churches is not merely the problem of liturgy, but the problem of leadership. The pastor has the choice between trying to make all decisions himself and trying to lead his parish, his *ekklesia* in miniature, into decisions. He has the choice between doing all the jobs himself and delegating them to others. He has the choice between teaching the Sunday school and guiding those who teach in the Sunday school. All too often, he acts as if he were the only Christian in the parish, and the natural result is that the parish consists of one harassed, overburdened Christian.

Leadership is never an easy matter, and in present-day America it has special frustrations and difficulties. There may have been a time when the leader was simply able to issue orders which were unquestioningly obeyed, as the centurion described it in his conversation with Christ in the Gospel, but today the delegation of a job includes, to a greater or lesser extent, a "dying" to the job. The person to whom the job is delegated must be trusted to understand its importance, to sense its purpose, to choose appropriate techniques, and to do the job in his own way.

The professional who delegates a job to an amateur must die a thousand deaths as he watches the amateur make mistakes which he, the professional, would know enough to avoid. It is easy to understand why the clergyman has an almost irresistible impulse to run the whole parish enterprise personally, using his laypeople merely as taxpayers and errand boys.

Yet the clergyman who succumbs to this concept of his work is harming his parish in more ways than one. There is the obvious fact that he could accomplish more if he knew how to delegate authority effectively. Equally obvious is the fact that he is standing in the way of his people's growth in the faith, their effective expression of the new life God pours into them at the baptismal font and the altar. But not quite so obvious, perhaps, is the much more serious fact that the clergy-dominated parish is a self-centered parish. Its goals get all tangled up with the pastor's personal goals. The work of God's Church becomes "church work."

This is the unspoken heresy that lies behind a vast amount of the thought and activity of the Church today. The Son of man came not to be ministered unto but to minister and to give His life as a ransom for many. The parish of today exists not to minister, but to be ministered unto, and it isn't going to give its life as a ransom for anybody. The parish has no real theological basis for existence except as the body of Christ. If it is not the body of Christ, it is nothing. And a self-centered body is not the body of Christ.

The notion is widespread today that there is something irreligious about being a layman. It is one of those taken-for-granted, unspoken assumptions that often provide more powerful motivations for actions and attitudes than formal ideas and beliefs. If a layman "gets religion," the obvious thing for him to do is to become a clergyman. Why?

The real problem is the "clericalism" of clergy and laity alike—the general acceptance of the idea that the clergy are the "real" Church, the only full-time practicing Christians. Too often, the clergy accept this concept of themselves and their role. In a world of teamwork, the parish priest frequently tries to be the whole team. Against this, the Church sets forth a very different relationship in its life of worship. There, every man has his "liturgy." Where the true "shape" of Christian worship is made manifest, the priest is not the deacon, the deacon is not the layman, and none of them can be dispensed with. The answer to clericalism is not laicism, but the ancient teamwork practiced by the Church long before the modern world discovered the fruitfulness of teamwork as a principle of organization in human affairs.

Almighty and everlasting God, by whose Spirit the whole body of the Church is governed and sanctified; Receive our supplications and prayers, which we offer before thee for all estates of men in thy holy Church, that every member of the same, in his vocation and ministry, may truly and godly serve thee; through our Lord and Saviour Jesus Christ. Amen.

Book of Common Prayer, page 156

* * 2 * *

What's Wrong with the World?

THE WORLD is a big place, and an even bigger idea. In the Bible and in Christian thought, "the world" means a number of different things, and the Christian is sometimes advised to turn away from it and sometimes advised to embrace it. We are told to be "in the world but not of it"; and we are also told that "God sent not his Son into the world to condemn the world; but that the world through him might be saved."

In such a context, however, the ambiguity does not lie in the fact that the word "world" sometimes means different things. The world we are called upon to love is the same world that we are called upon to reject—the world of men and nations, of civilization and culture, of farms and factories and wars and all things human. This is the world in which "the Son of man came not to be ministered unto but to minister, and to give his life a ransom for many."

The Christian attitude toward this world is ambiguous because the world is in the grip of its own internal conflicts. The passage just quoted from St. Mark

10:45 is a good example. It was Jesus' reply to the request of James and John for a worldly type of recognition of their efforts on behalf of His kingdom. He told them that their goal in following Him was not to be power or success or glory, but service and self-sacrifice. They were to deal with the world not in terms of the world's values but in terms of an altogether different set of values.

The world needs to be served and saved. This was true of first-century Palestine, and it is true of modern America. It is true of Soviet Russia and Red China. There are no boundaries to the ministry of Christ, nor to the work of the Church of Christ. Wherever people are found, there the Church ought to be seeking and saving.

A generation ago, the Christian view of the human predicament was widely challenged. Science, education, and industrial progress seemed to be well on the way to solving all human problems, and those who said that there was a fundamental twist in human nature which was bound to frustrate our efforts at self-improvement found it hard to get a hearing.

The idea that the best minds of modern science would be indentured to the government for the production of engines of destruction had not occurred to anybody then. Nor had the discussion of education come to focus, as it has today, upon enhancing the nation's war-making power. Something called "enlightened self-interest" was set forth as the moral principle to be followed by any man in search of the good life.

But the level-headed citizen of today cannot even object to the acceptance of war-making power as the central goal of our political and social life. There is no alternative, except the alternative of knuckling under to police states which shamelessly make war upon their own defenseless citizens.

In other words, sin has become a fact to be reckoned with. Our danger today is not unconsciousness of sin, but the notion that our sins would be no problem if other people's sins—for example, the Russians'—did not poison the atmosphere. Sin looms large in relations between management and labor, between government and citizen, between employer and employee, between husband and wife, between parent and child. And in these relationships, as in the great problems of international affairs, earnest exhortations to live sinlessly seem quite beside the point.

Our literary figures preach a philosophy of "acceptance." This philosophy is dramatized by a "beat generation" dedicated to showing the world what unlovely specimens it must accept. Those who still speak up for cultural and moral values try to do so in terms of "maturity"—of not being surprised or hurt to find that these values are not the key to instant success.

To confuse the situation perfectly, God has loosed upon modern America a barrage of plenty beyond the wildest dreams of earlier ages. Obesity, not famine, is today's food problem. Big car *vs.* little car is the central issue in the family council. As we groan under our tax burden, we buy TV sets, refrigerators, washing machines, power mowers, new houses, new clothes, books, newspapers, magazines, art objects, do-it-yourself tools—the list is endless.

But none of these things is the key to happiness, nor even to contentment. None of these things prevents the breakup of families or decreases the juvenile delinquency statistics or assuages the gnawing anxieties that afflict our age.

Almighty God, who seest that we have no power of ourselves to help ourselves; Keep us both outwardly in our bodies, and inwardly in our souls; that we may be defended from all adversities which may happen to the body, and from all evil thoughts which may assault and hurt the soul; through Jesus Christ our Lord. Amen.

Book of Common Prayer, page 127

* * * * *

Not long ago, it was reported that an alarming trend was in evidence among homing pigeons. They seemed to be losing their homing instinct. On routine flights that should be no problem to a homing pigeon, 90%, 95%, or even 100% failed to reach their homes. Scientists speculated on the possible causes—speculations which were somewhat hampered by the fact that nobody knows what causes the homing instinct in the first place.

This trend is not reported as another "sign of the times." Pigeons have their own problems, which are undoubtedly different from those of humans. Yet a homing pigeon that has lost its homing instinct is a good illustration of the condition of mankind.

The mystery of the homing faculty once had and then lost suggests comparison with mankind's initial state of grace, the loss of which is known as original sin. Like the pigeons, we were created with a destiny, a destination. Heaven was our home, and we were endowed with a native ability to find it.

Christianity does not assert that man in his primitive state was wise, or civilized, or cultured, or brilliant, but only that he was "homing man," able to detect and follow the signs and signals that led him to heaven. The calamitous loss of this faculty was, the Bible indicates, due to a willful following of signals that had a different origin. And once the way home had become obscure, man had lost the central principle of his whole existence.

A lost homing pigeon is just another waif of the public parks, laying its eggs on the precarious ledges of courthouses and city halls. One might imagine such a pigeon stirred by the homeward pull for a time, but little by little learning to ignore it, and finally coming to doubt that there had ever been such a place as home; or, if there be such a place, no longer even desiring to get there.

So it is with fallen mankind. There is an abiding nostalgia within us, but we are not sure that it is for any real place; and if there be such a place as heaven, our desire for it is so faint that a thousand and one other objectives seem more urgent and immediate.

Actual sins, our daily misdoings in thought, word, and deed, are the product of our failure to understand our supernatural destiny and to move toward our heavenly destination. Fending for ourselves in an indifferent world, we find an endless succession of very good reasons for satisfying our earth-centered hungers first and thinking about God second.

Christ does not come to us with a long list of do's and don't's, assuring us that the man who follows them will earn God's approval. He comes to replant in us our original homing instinct, to recall us to the goal of union with Him. He comes to remind us of the kingdom of heaven and to draw us to love and worship of the King. Then "all these things will be added unto you." The first thing a homing pigeon needs is to get his homing apparatus in working order again.

Just as a well-fed pigeon on the courthouse steps is still a waif of the pigeon world, so a well-fed, well-housed, well-clad American is still a lost, strayed, or stolen child of the kingdom of heaven. Original sin is not our desire to be healthy, happy, and famous, but our loss of understanding of an ultimate destiny which includes and transcends health, happiness, and fame.

Once that goal is lost from our inward sight, all the lesser goods that men aspire to become temptations. We think, or hope, they will satisfy our internal hunger for God; and they do, temporarily at least, remove it from the center of our attention.

And our attention is important. Walter Farrell, commenting on the *Summa Theologica* of St. Thomas Aquinas, explains how the angels were able to sin even though nothing bad existed in the spiritual universe. God had given them the ability to contemplate and appreciate their own moral beauty and excellence, since the ability to rejoice in creation is a part of the spiritual equipment of every rational creature. (When the world was made, the Bible says, "the sons of God shouted for joy.") But the angels were able to contemplate only one thing at a time. Those that chose to continue to contemplate themselves unceasingly, never lifting their attention to God, turned their own good into sin by making it a barrier between themselves and their reason for being.

Similarly, in the affairs of men, every good thing can become a barrier between us and our reason for being. And since the universal condition of mankind without

Christ is a condition of separation from our reason for being, the likelihood is small that we can find God by seeking togetherness or maturity or culture or good-neighborliness. The Thirty-Nine Articles in the back of the Prayer Book put it in uncompromising sixteenth-century terms (*Article XIII*): "Works done before the grace of Christ, and the Inspiration of His Spirit, are not pleasant to God, forasmuch as they spring not of faith in Jesus Christ; neither do they make men meet to receive grace, or (as the School-authors say) deserve grace of congruity; yea rather, for that they are not done as God hath willed and commanded them to be done, we doubt not but they have the nature of sin."

Is this the condition of the world? Must we follow along with the Thirty-Nine Articles and say that even the good deeds of non-Christians "have the nature of sin"? Theologians generally have their escape hatches from rigorous statements like this, and you will be doing no worse than the "School-authors"—i.e., the medieval philosophers of whom Aquinas was the brightest star—if you find a twentieth-century style escape hatch of your own. You can speculate that Mahatma Gandhi, for instance, must have had some of the grace of Christ and the inspiration of His Spirit. Or you can jump over the Thirty-Nine Articles back to the scholastics and say that good deeds which do not come to focus on mankind's eternal destiny are still pleasing to God in that Christ Himself has declared that those who feed the hungry, clothe the naked, visit the prisoners, and welcome the strangers have performed a service for Him.

But the thing to keep in mind is that attention is important. The angels fell because they were so busy in a good work that they never got around to a better one. The long-range value of any good deed must be related to its significance as a movement toward knowing and loving God.

O God of peace, who hast taught us that in returning and rest we shall be saved, in quietness and in confidence shall be our strength; By the might of thy Spirit lift us, we pray thee, to thy presence, where we may be still and know that thou art God; through Jesus Christ our Lord. Amen.

Book of Common Prayer, page 595

❋ ❋ ❋ ❋ ❋

So, the vast world of mankind sprawls out before us, a world of lost creatures who are by no means certain that such a thing as home has ever existed. Some of them are busy trying to help each other to get from nowhere to nowhere, others are busy trying to beat somebody else to nowhere, or are merely trying to enjoy life in the nowhere they presently inhabit.

The Son of man came to seek and save that which is lost. The Son of man came not to be ministered unto but to minister, and to give His life a ransom for many. Who carries on that mission today? The clergy? The laity? Or the whole Church?

And the question is not only "Who?" but "How?" By argument? Perhaps some very intellectual person is occasionally won to faith in Christ by argument. By preaching? Some people seem to be won to Christ by preaching. But, like the sacraments, the normal place of preaching seems to be within the fellowship of the Church rather than out in the market place. Even those stirred to decision by the great public evangelistic campaigns commonly turn out to be people who are already fairly active members of some Christian Church. Through good works—hospitals, settlements, counseling services, relief programs, community activities, public affairs forums, and the like? Yes, these too occasionally serve as means of manifesting the face of Christ.

The real "how," of course, is the grace of God working invisibly in each human soul. And yet God has so organized the world that we who are already Christians are an indispensable link in the making of new Christians. We constitute an ongoing community, extending down the ages, bearing such witness as our failings do not nullify to the life that is in us. Only by the grace of God can a man recognize the face of Christ shining forth from ordinary Christians. But that is virtually the only place in the whole world where the face of Christ can be found.

Bible, sacraments, creeds, and apostolic ministry are controlling features of the life of the Church. These are the four points highlighted by Anglicanism as the basis for discussions of unity with other Churches. But all of these—including the ministry—belong to the internal life of the Church much more than to its impact on the world.

In one of Chesterton's Father Brown stories, the little priest became involved in an afternoon walk with a man he suspected of being the notorious criminal Flambeau disguised as a fellow-priest. Father Brown left behind him a trail of extraordinary circumstances. In a restaurant, salt in the sugar bowl and sugar in the salt-cellar. On a fruit stand, switched labels and price tags. In another restaurant, Father Brown broke a window and paid for the privilege on the spot. Wherever the two went that afternoon, something peculiar happened. The upshot was that the great French detective pursuing Flambeau followed the trail of the peculiar because he had nothing else to follow and caught up with the pair in the nick of time.

Something of this detective story character invests St. Mark's account of "the Gospel of Jesus Christ, the Son of God." In this case, the "something peculiar" has to do with the nature of the cosmic culprit whom St. Mark invites the reader to trail.

The story begins with John the Baptist, preaching in the wilderness of Judea. Everybody, but everybody, went out to see him—"all the country of Judea, and all the people of Jerusalem," says the author. But when one man came to be baptized something strange happened. He saw the heavens opened, the spirit descending like a dove; heard a voice: "Thou art my beloved Son; with thee I am well pleased." St. Mark doesn't let us know whether anybody other than Jesus saw or heard this; the other evangelists tell about that. But after the forty days in the wilderness, after the gathering of some disciples, things began to happen. Our suspect taught in the synagogue at Capernaum, astonishing everybody with His authority. A crazy man made a strange remark on that occasion: "What have you to do with us, Jesus of Nazareth? Have you come to destroy us?" And Jesus ordered the devil to come out of the man, and it did. "Immediately," says St. Mark, He left the synagogue, went to the house of one of His disciples, and cured the man's mother-in-law of a fever. That evening, when the day's work was over, they brought all the sick and demon-possessed to Him, and He healed them. And so things went on. "He went throughout all Galilee, preaching in their synagogues and casting out demons." More examples are given: the leper, who went around talking about his good fortune so much that Jesus had to stay out in the country until things quieted down. The paralytic, let down through a hole in the roof because he couldn't be brought through the crowds into the house where Jesus was. The man who had a withered hand; he healed this man on the Sabbath, demonstrating to the Pharisees that "the Son of Man is lord even of the Sabbath."

St. Mark scatters other clues around. In the case of the paralytic, Jesus began by saying that the man's sins were forgiven, and made His words good by the healing. But the thing which the evangelist keeps driving home about the subject of *the* Gospel is that everywhere He went He naturally, inevitably, almost uncontrollably, spread *some* gospel: some good news, some restoration of health or sanity or self-respect. For right in the midst of the other marvels appears the story of Jesus consorting with the tax collectors and sinners, to the amazement of the scribes and Pharisees.

Who is this man? What is this man? Telling how Jesus stopped a storm on the lake, St. Mark actually puts the question in words: "Who then is this, that even wind and sea obey him?"

The Christian Church has answered this question to its satisfaction, beginning with Peter's Confession on the road to Caesarea Philippi, and continuing with the apostolic preaching, the writing of the New Testament, the formulation of the creeds, and the evangelization of nations and continents. He is "the Christ, the Son of the living God."

This business of "some gospel," of miraculous works of compassion and mercy, is a rather distinctive feature of Christianity. Mohammed never did anything like it. Gautama Buddha, we are told, considered it and rejected it for his high, austere way which later generations accommodated to the exigencies of a superstitious mankind.

The Christian Gospel has the unique quality of being compressible into one characteristic, redemptive act, such as sitting down with a notorious grafter or curing an old woman of the flu. It is not a masterpiece of statecraft nor a general philosophical explanation of how the world began and how it will end. It is "a light shining in the darkness," and a strong enough light also to shine in that gray twilight that characterizes our humanistic, Christian-influenced world.

The thing that made Christ's miracles so dramatic to the world of His time was not their magical character. It was a world in which strange things were happening to everybody all the time. St. Luke hits the right note exactly in his account of Christ's first preaching at the synagogue in Nazareth:

"He opened the book and found the place where it was written: 'The spirit of the Lord is upon me, because he has anointed me to preach good news to the poor. He has sent me to proclaim release to the captives and recovering of sight to the blind, to set at liberty those that are oppressed, to proclaim the acceptable year of the Lord'. . . . and he began to say to them, 'today this Scripture has been fulfilled in your hearing.' "

The manner of deliverance to the poor, the captives, the blind, the oppressed, was secondary to the fact of their deliverance. A rabbi, a teacher, a prophet did not ordinarily spend his time in the slums. His *metier* should be refined colloquy with the spiritually athletic—better news for people to whom the news from the battlefront of the soul was already pretty good.

St. Luke also records the answer to the disciples of St. John the Baptist, who were sent to ask, "Are you he who is to come, or shall we look for another?" Jesus' answer was: "Go and tell John what you have seen and heard: the blind receive their sight, the lame walk, lepers are cleansed, and the deaf hear, the dead are raised up, the poor have good news preached to them. And blessed is he who takes no offense at me."

It is also in accord with the ideas of the Gospel to spiritualize these human needs and their fulfillment by Christ. The beatitudes, in St. Matthew's version, for example, refer to the "poor *in spirit*," and those who "hunger and thirst *after righteousness*," where St. Luke refers simply to the poor and the hungry. Jesus Himself not only spoke of spiritual blindness and deafness but directly connected His physical healings with the spiritual forgiveness of sins. Both the physical and the spiritual are within the realm of God's concern and of Christ's redemptive action. Either the physical or the spiritual is capable of being the medium for the manifestation of *the* good news through an action that brings *some* good news.

Almighty God, who didst inspire thy servant Saint Luke the Physician, to set forth in the Gospel the love and healing power of thy Son; Manifest in thy Church the like power and love, to the healing of our bodies and our souls; through the same thy Son Jesus Christ our Lord. Amen.

Book of Common Prayer, page 253

* * * * *

Accordingly, when Christianity goes out into the world of today "to seek and save that which is lost," it does not need to go out with its full panoply of bishops, Bible, sacraments, creeds, theology, philosophy, psychology, sociology, political science, and business acumen. It does not need polished evangelistic techniques, nor miracles. It needs only to have an eye for meeting some genuine need of some genuine human being. These other items may be useful, and some of them are essential items in the resources of the Church. But when it comes to an encounter with the world, a cup of cold water given in the name of Christ is the sacramental vehicle, the characteristic piece of good news, the sample of Gospel, which implies all the rest.

Joseph Fletcher, the distinguished professor of Christian Ethics, describes such Christian encounters with humanity as "paradigmatic acts"—acts which illustrate the meaning of the Gospel, as the paradigm noun or verb illustrates principles of grammar.

The performance of such "paradigmatic acts" is the central ministry of the laity. And such actions are the Church's main means of proclaiming the Gospel to the world. The business man in his office, the housewife shopping for a new dress, the prizefighter in the ring, the checkout girl in the supermarket, the bootblack on the corner—each member of the body of Christ, wherever he may be, is constantly called upon to carry forward the work of the Church through his or her peculiarly Christian response to the circumstances in which he is placed.

Each time a Christian comes into contact with another human being, he comes to a moment of judgment of his relationship with Christ. "Lord, when did we see thee hungry and feed thee, or thirsty and give thee drink? And when did we see thee sick or in prison and visit thee?" "Truly, I say to you, as you did it to one of the least of these my brethren, you did it to me."

So Christ declared His identification with those He came to serve. "Homing man" does not regain his original relationship to God in solitude, but in a homeward-bound flock. And since it is a flock of men, rather than pigeons, it has a peculiarly human "ecology," a relationship of love, mutual help, compassion, and self-giving which follows the paradigm of Christ's own life and ministry. Christ shows us what humanity really is, as both the subject and the object of Christian charity. When we love our neighbor, Christ in us loves our neighbor; when we love our neighbor, we love Christ; and thus it is that the world of men encounters Christ and through Him begins to be conformed to the kingdom of heaven.

Almighty God, who hast poured upon us the new light of thine incarnate Word; *Grant that the same light enkindled in our hearts may shine forth in our lives; through Jesus Christ our Lord.* Amen.

Book of Common Prayer, page 106

* * 3 * *

What's Wrong with the Parish?

THE ONLY KIND of Christianity that effectively exists is parochial Christianity. It is the only kind that ever has existed or ever will exist, except for some transitional or tributary forms of church life deriving their significance and vitality from their relationship to local congregations.

The rediscovery of the fact that man lives as part of a community rather than as a solitary individual is not easy for modern Americans to accept. In the secular realm, such books as *The Organization Man,* by William H. Whyte, Jr., *The Hidden Persuaders* and *The Status Seekers,* by Vance Packard, report the way we are influenced by, and hierarchically related to, our fellows with an air of exposing an alien cancer in the body of society.

In fact, the rugged self-determined individual has always been pretty much of a myth. To the extent that such men have existed at all, they were the end product of a society which taught them what to eat, how to speak, how to find shelter from the elements, how to read books and listen to music, how to pray, and how to make love. We are not insects, supplied with a built-in set of instincts adequate to every occasion. We are the products of teaching and learning, inheritors of a culture, social beings who are still the products of society when we turn our backs on society to contemplate the mental and spiritual gifts society has lavished upon us.

There is no such thing as a man without a community, a culture, a language, a relationship to other men and women. And there is no such thing as a Christian man without a Christian congregation. It is no accident that the central action enjoined upon us by Christ for expressing and renewing our relationship with Him is called Holy Communion. The word St. Paul used for "Communion" was "*Koinonia*"—the act of using something in common. It is sometimes translated as "fellowship." And "*koinonia*" had the same down-to-earth connotations as our word "common." St. Peter used the adjective "*koinos*" when he said that he had never eaten anything "common or unclean."

Christianity is a matter of common people engaging in common prayer and participating in a common life. Although the structure of the local church may vary widely to adapt to changing cultural conditions or to reflect historical developments, the congregation is just as truly of the *esse*, the essential nature, of the Church as the episcopate is.

In a little sermon addressed to new members of the Church who were receiving their first Communion, the great St. Augustine of Hippo sketched the meaning of their Christian initiation in terms of what happens to a grain of wheat in the process of being incorporated into a loaf of bread:

"You ought to know what you have received, what you are going to receive, and what you ought to receive daily. That Bread, which you see on the altar, consecrated by the word of God, is the body of Christ. That chalice, or rather, what the chalice holds, consecrated by the word of God, is the Blood of Christ. . . . If you have received worthily, you are what you have received, for the Apostle says: 'The bread is one; we, though many are one body. . . .' So, by bread, you are instructed as to how you ought to cherish unity.

"Was that bread made of one grain of wheat? Were there not, rather, many grains? However, before they became bread, these grains were separate; they were joined together in water after a certain amount of crushing. For unless the grain is ground and moistened with water, it cannot arrive at that form which is called bread. So, too, you were previously ground, as it were, by the humiliation of your fasting and by the sacrament of exorcism. Then came the baptism of water; you were moistened, as it were, so as to arrive at the form of bread.

"But, without fire, bread does not yet exist. What then, does the fire signify? The chrism [Confirmation]. For the sacrament of the Holy Spirit is the oil of our fire. . . . He enkindles charity by which we ardently desire God and spurn the world, by which our chaff is consumed and our heart purified as gold. Therefore, the fire, that is, the Holy Spirit, comes after the water; then you become bread, that is, the body of Christ. . . .

"Receive, then, so that you may ponder, so that you may always possess unity in your heart, so that you may always lift up your heart. . . ."

Union with God is no flight of the alone to the Alone,

the reception of the sacrament is not a solitary encounter of the soul with Christ. We are saved into a community, and in a community, and our union and communion is with each other as well as with Christ.

Almighty God, who hast given us grace at this time with one accord to make our common supplications unto thee; and dost promise that when two or three are gathered together in thy Name thou wilt grant their requests; Fulfil now, O Lord, the desires and petitions of thy servants, as may be most expedient for them; granting us in this world knowledge of thy truth, and in the world to come life everlasting. Amen.

Book of Common Prayer, page 20

What is the state of the Christian congregation in modern America? Is it the "one loaf" described by St. Augustine, ground and moistened and transformed by fire into nourishing food for the whole world? The observations which follow are concerned specifically with the Episcopal Church because it is important to be specific about this subject. Americans cannot be won to Christ by a theoretical Christian fellowship but only by Christian fellowships that actually exist. The reader who belongs to another Christian communion must judge for himself whether the Christian fellowship he knows faces similar problems.

In the Episcopal Church in modern America, the local Christian community in which the great events of salvation take place is the parish, with its rector, wardens, and vestrymen, its choir and acolytes and altar guild and men's and women's groups, its church and educational building and rectory, its every member canvass, its building committee, and all its associated activities and appurtenances. These are the saints on Main Street, and this is the contemporary communion (Koinonia) of saints.

From the standpoint of the dynamics of the kingdom of God, where the parish is, there is the Church of Christ. There isn't any other place for it to be except in similar congregations of other Christian communions.

And yet, the parish in twentieth-century America is commonly far removed from any conscious or purposeful dedication to the redemption of the secular community in which it lives. In Chapter 1 it was stated that "the parish of today exists not to minister, but to be ministered unto, and it isn't going to give its life as a ransom for anybody."

This is a great period of prosperity in the life of the parishes. Most of them are growing according to every index of success. Their membership is on the rise, the Sunday school is bursting at the seams, old debts are being paid off, new ones are easily floated for ambitious new building projects, men and women are active in parish groups, financial contributions are increasing, and people are praying, studying, and working harder than ever before.

There is, however, a curiously introverted quality about the entire enterprise. Typically, the parish measures its progress not according to the norms of its service to community and world, but according to the norms of its own size and financial strength. Similarly, it measures the usefulness of its members not by their service to community and world but by their service to the parish itself.

Success standards such as these are the standards of a secular club or fraternal association. They have a good deal in common with the request of James and John to Jesus: "Grant us to sit, one at your right hand and one at your left, in your glory."

The parish of today—especially the vigorous, optimistic parish springing up like a mushroom in modern suburbia—is typically in the grip of a godless dynamism. It is, as someone has said "of the world, but not in it." It can get excited about suburban affairs when it has an institutional stake in a zoning problem or in a proposal to assess non-profit corporations for fire and police services. It can get roused up about "combatting juvenile delinquency" when it sees an opportunity to lure respectable young people into youth activities that may lead toward capturing them as members. But unless the parish sees some gain to itself as an institution in a particular course of action, it is unlikely to do anything about it.

The vigor and vitality of which the parish is capable when it is seeking its own ends is truly phenomenal. It is one of the leading success-institutions of our day, and merely to be given a place in the lower echelons of its leadership is a valuable bit of recognition for a fortunate man or woman trying to put down roots in a new community. The only thing missing is those outgoing, paradigmatic actions which would make the world suspect the presence of its Saviour in the parish.

Actually, welcoming the new member of the community and quickly assimilating him into a role of importance is one of the genuinely Christian, truly paradigmatic things the parish does. Welcome wagons and door-to-door charitable campaigns do their bit to meet this human need, but the parish does it better, faster, and on a broader front.

Such a parish is in the grip of a godless dynamism not because it is godless, but because the forces which drive it into action have little to do with God's ends. When James and John laid claim to a position of honor at the side of the Lord in glory, they were not denying their faith in Him—quite the contrary. They were just mixed up about the implications of their faith for their personal goals and activities.

There are many other parishes in which the problem is not godless dynamism but godless feebleness and frustration. The membership list may be static or declining, the Sunday school may be puny, money may be hard to come by, the church building may be getting shabbier and shabbier. Anxiety about failure according to the world's standards can be just as intense a preoccupation as a frenetic drive toward success. Such a parish cannot lift up its head to look at its mission in the community and world because it is so busy trying to keep itself alive.

But such a parish is under as heavy an obligation as the strong, vital, successful parish to exhibit to its members and to the world around it the good news of Jesus Christ. No parish has to be prosperous, no parish even has to survive. All it has to do is to follow its Lord, relying on His promise that He will give it provision according to its needs. Until the parish is able to look beyond its internal concerns to the need of the world, it is no better off, from the divine standpoint, in prosperity than in adversity.

Grant, we beseech thee, merciful Lord, to thy faithful people pardon and peace, that they may be cleansed from all their sins, and serve thee with a quiet mind; through Jesus Christ our Lord. Amen.

Book of Common Prayer, page 218

The root problem of the parish today, whether rich or poor, strong or weak, is, of course, a problem of its members. If it has become involved in the world's standards of success, the reason is that the world sits on the vestry—and it often wears a clerical collar. A young pastor, fresh out of seminary, may have high ideas about the scope of the Church's redemptive task, but as he gets a little older and more experienced he finds that somebody has to worry about membership and money and parish activities and physical plant and all the other down-to-earth realities of parish life. He finds that nobody is quite as unbusinesslike as a businessman on the vestry, and that one of his unending tasks is to persuade laymen to be practical.

It is only natural that the experienced professional in religion would take a professional point of view and the amateur would be somewhat amateurish. But a part of our confusion about the functions of clergy and laity is the assumption that the clergyman is the spokesman for religion in the parish and the layman the spokesman for worldly wisdom. The layman on the vestry is likely to spend a lot of time advancing impractical schemes to solve the parish's financial problems, about which the clergyman knows a great deal more than he does, opposing expenditures that cannot be avoided, or dreaming of income that cannot be obtained. This is the posture demanded of him by our mental stereotypes of the "hard-headed layman."

If instead, the layman audited the parish's business from the standpoint of what the Church was doing for his next-door neighbor, for his business associate, for the sore spot in community relations represented by a slum area, for all his fellow laypeople in all settings and circumstances, then he would be really representing the laity in the central planning of the parish.

And he would be talking about an area in which his qualifications might well exceed those of the parish priest.

The stereotype of the hard-headed priest and the soft-hearted layman is, of course, no more generally valid than the reverse stereotype. Either a priest or a layman can be aware of the needs of suffering humanity. Either a priest or a layman can be a devoted Christian, just as a professional baseball player may like baseball better than many of the people who have paid to come to the game.

The real question is: Who is going to recall the parish to the central purpose defined by its Lord: Ministering to mankind, not being ministered unto, and giving its life a ransom for many?

This is Christ's definition of His own mission, and theologians can argue shrewdly that what Christ said and did cannot invariably be transferred to His followers as the model for their own behavior. But in this particular case the theologians' argument is with Jesus Himself, for His express purpose in so defining His mission was to point out that His followers were obliged to act accordingly.

If everybody in the parish leadership is being parish-centered, nobody is left to speak up for the Gospel: neither the priest nor the layman.

Clergy and laity alike, we are all men under judgment. To us individually as parishioners, parish leaders, vestrymen, clergymen, or bishops will be addressed the stern reminder of Christ at the Last Judgment that judgment day for each of us actually came and went a long time ago: "Lord, when did we see thee hungry or thirsty or a stranger or naked or sick or in prison, and did not minister to thee?"

And if this is a question for each individual, clerical and lay, it is also a corporate question for the corporate body of the parish. Rector, wardens, and vestrymen, not only individually but corporately, must redirect the godless dynamism of their group life into the kind of activity that is appropriate to God-centered man.

"A city that is set on a hill cannot be hid," said Christ in the Sermon on the Mount. "Let your light so shine before men, that they may see your good works, and glorify your Father which is in heaven." This last sentence is used as one of the offertory sentences in the church service and is undoubtedly thought of as an exhortation to give money to the Church. But Jesus was speaking here of the Church's witness to the world. The good works He referred to were those paradigmatic acts which would reveal the glory and love and mercy of God to lost and groping humanity.

It is the task of priest and people alike, and of the parish corporately, "to preach good news to the poor, to proclaim release to the captives and recovering of sight to the blind, to set at liberty those that are oppressed," not merely in terms of some grand scheme for a better social order, nor in the promise of a great future consummation of history, but in those paradigmatic actions, those daily testimonies to God's continuing love and concern which, like the healings of Jesus, meet today's needs for the men and women of today.

O Lord, who has taught us that all our doings without charity are nothing worth; Send thy Holy Ghost, and pour into our hearts that most excellent gift of charity, the very bond of peace and of all virtues, without which whosoever liveth is counted dead before thee. Grant this for thine only Son Jesus Christ's sake. Amen.

Book of Common Prayer, page 122

In the art of public relations, much attention is currently being given to the "image" the business firm and its products present to the public. Here again, the layman involved in parish leadership has a valuable lay contribution to make. What kind of "image" does the parish present to those outside it? Caution must, of course, be used in applying such a question to the life of the Church. The parish has no ultimate obligation to be the kind of institution the world understands and accepts. Rather, its obligation is to be the kind of institution that shows the world what God is like as He is revealed to us in Jesus Christ. Part of the time, Jesus was very popular; but not all the time. The good works enjoined upon us by our Christian vocation are not those which will make the Church appear to be something it is not, but those which will demonstrate what the Church is.

It is not easy for the parish priest to find out what sort of image his church presents to the community, and it is even harder for him to do anything about clarifying and strengthening it. This is a job for the laity.

The most central witness which the parish gives the world about the nature of the Church of Christ, however, is in the relationships among its own members. As the public relations men say, you can't do too much about the external public relations of an industrial firm unless its internal public relations are in good shape. Unless Christians love each other, they are going to find it very difficult to exhibit the love of God to the world.

St. John's account of Jesus' Prayer at the Last Supper expresses this idea very simply: "I do not pray for these only, but also for those who are to believe in me through their word, that they may all be one; even as thou, Father, art in me, and I in thee, that they also may be in us, so that the world may believe that thou hast sent me."

This passage is frequently quoted with reference to the relationships between different communions of Christians, and it is highly relevant there. But its more direct and immediate application, then as now, was to the relationships existing among the members of the local Christian congregation.

Christians can fall into unchristian feuding over some remarkably insignificant questions: whether the church door should be painted red; whether one location or another should be chosen for a new building; whether one or another kind of dishwasher should be used in the new kitchen; whether professional fund-raising counsel should be employed; whether pews or cathedral chairs should be purchased; whether there should be a genuflexion during the Nicene Creed; whether a sanctus bell should be used. There are bigger issues for which it is easier to justify controversy, and sometimes issues arise on which controversy is inevitable. The New Testament gives plenty of evidence that life was not always serene in the parishes of the early Church.

Nevertheless, every issue that comes up in the parish ought to be viewed first of all as an opportunity for the exercise of Christian love, Christian forgiveness, Christain forbearance. Usually the man who will fight to the death on an insignificant issue is doing so on behalf of some great principle. The question is whether an even greater principle, the principle of brotherly love, might not moderate his warfare with his fellow-Christians.

In the vestry, in the guild, in questions about vestments and music and ceremonial, the first problem is to make the parish *look* and *sound* and *act* like the Church of Christ because it *is* the Church of Christ. Agreement may not always be possible, but love is always possible. We must learn to look upon our fellow-parishioners as persons first and opponents (or allies) second. The question, "What will this decision do for the parish?" must also be faced in terms of what it will do to lackadaisical John Jones or argumentative Mary Smith. He or she may be the one who is hungry, or thirsty, or a stranger, or naked, or sick, or in prison, in terms of the hunger and defenselessness and bondage that afflict the soul; he or she may be the one about whom Christ will inquire on judgment day.

The time for Christianity to bear fruit is today, not tomorrow. This theme runs constantly through the preaching of Christ. The plan being developed by the planning group cannot possibly be big enough and Christian enough to justify an unchristian spirit or unchristian actions within the group. The smallest action that is truly paradigmatic of the Gospel here and now is more important in the kingdom of God than the grandest strategy for the future that the mind can conceive.

The world, after all, is in the hands of God. He does not need money, nor church buildings, nor missionary programs, nor Sunday schools. He does not even need parishes, vestries, guilds, and discussion groups. There is nothing we can do either to advance or retard the coming of His kingdom. He gives us our little areas of importance for our sakes, not for His. What we do with our projects is entirely secondary to the spirit in which we tackle them.

The Christian helping God is like a four-year-old child helping to weed the garden. He will probably do nearly as much harm as good, but it is good for him to be helpful.

O Almighty and most merciful God, of thy bountiful goodness keep us, we beseech thee, from all things that may hurt us; that we, being ready both in body and soul, may cheerfully accomplish those things which thou commandest; through Jesus Christ our Lord. Amen.

Book of Common Prayer, page 217

"Let your light so shine before men, that they may see your good works, and glorify your Father which is in heaven." A passerby seeing father and four-year-old working in the garden together probably would think well of the two, sensing the warmth of their relationship with each other.

The use of this text at the Offertory in the service of Holy Communion, although it has very little to do with "giving money to the Church," has everything to do with the real significance of the Offertory. An ancient term for the laymen participating in the Church's worship is *prospherontes*—"offerers." The bread and wine placed upon the altar constitute the main elements of the offering. And at this point in the service they represent the lives and the work of the people. In a growing number of our parishes today this important part of the dynamics of the Communion service is highlighted by having each person place a wafer in a ciborium (a cup-like vessel) as he comes in the church door. Then, at the time of the Offertory, the church wardens or other representative laymen bring up the bread and wine, the offering of the people, from the back of the church to the altar steps.

"Ye are the light of the world," said Jesus. What we have to offer represents our stewardship of the Light that is in us. During the week, at home, at work, in recreation, in our social and political life, in casual personal contacts and in civic and fraternal associations, we have had the opportunity to permit the Light of Christ to shine out so that men might see it and glorify our heavenly Father and His. Luckily for us, God did not accept us for our record of transparency to His Light. He accepted us as we were, and continues to accept our marred and cloudy offering of ourselves as a part of Christ's offering of Himself.

If mankind's service to God stopped short at an offertory, there would be no hope of salvation for anyone, for man is not able to save himself. There is no bank account on which we can draw to make good our repeated overdrafts upon His mercy. But the Holy Communion is our response to His initiative. The Offertory leads on into the Prayer of Consecration in which our offering is made a part of the offering of Him whose life was given as "a ransom for many." Jesus Christ Himself is what we offer to the Father; Jesus Christ is what the Father gives to us for our spiritual food so that we may be made one body with Christ and He may dwell in us and we in Him.

The parish is the place where we are incorporated into the body of Christ through baptism, and the place where we express and renew our relationship with Him in the Holy Communion—the parish, that is, as the Christian congregation, the local unit of the kingdom of God. To the extent that it is a full and vital unit of that kingdom, it will be aware of, and active in, the larger relationships of the Church—the diocese, area, or synod, the national Church, the Church throughout the world, the work of cooperation and the search for unity with the members of Christ in other Christian communions. But all these things begin within the parish at the altar of God. They are relationships "in Christ," not alliances with other like-minded men.

By the same token, because the parish *is* the Church,

it cannot leave missions to missionaries or social service to social workers. When these things are regarded as outside interests in competition with more immediate intraparochial concerns, the parish may say, like the Church of the Laodicians, "I am rich, I have prospered, and I need nothing," but in the eyes of God it is "wretched, pitiable, poor, blind, and naked."

In recent years, many noteworthy projects have been developed to express the concern of Christian people with the needs of the world. Agencies for Christian social service operate settlement houses, counselling services, institutions for the care of the aged and of children, and tackle many other community needs. But unless such institutions are supported by the parishes on a broad and vigorous basis, they seem to the world to represent, not a natural expression of the Church's inner nature but an eccentricity of a few, a peripheral concern foisted upon the Church by the power of their nagging insistence.

The parish of today is inescapably involved in social relations. It is a social institution living in a social setting from which it could not escape if it tried. The question is not whether it will have social relations, but whether these relationships will be Christian—whether, in the things it says and does in its encounters with the world, it will give expression to "some gospel," will allow a ray of the Light of Christ to shine forth from its heart.

This task cannot be a side-issue, the responsibility of a committee consisting of those who have a special interest in charitable enterprises or social theory. It must be a central responsibility of the effective parish leadership, clerical and lay, as high on the agenda as the Sunday school, the maintenance of the parish plant, and the every member canvass.

No doubt an off-beat social relations interest is better than none. Christ told us to bother God with our prayers in His parable of the unjust judge who neither feared God nor regarded man, but granted the widow's petition just to get rid of her. And bothering the parish with missionary and social appeals is one way of accomplishing Christian objectives.

Yet it is to be hoped that the next decade will see a rebirth of missionary and social concern in this country of comparable scope to the rebirth of concern with Christian education which has characterized the past decade. We know today that the parish without a vigorous program for educating children in the faith is a dead or dying parish. Ten years hence we may know that the parish without a vigorous program for advancing the Church's mission in community and world is also a dead or dying parish.

Lord, we beseech thee to keep thy household the Church in continual godliness; that through thy protection it may be free from all adversities, and devoutly given to serve thee in good works, to the glory of thy Name; through Jesus Christ our Lord. Amen.

Book of Common Prayer, page 220

* * 4 * *

Rediscovering the Gospel

THERE IS something about the world of our times which makes the Gospel more of a live issue for people at all intellectual levels than it has been for many years. All through European and American history, religion has been regarded as a good thing and the Christian religion has been regarded as the right one for Western man. But "religion" is a very large and inclusive concept. "The Gospel" is a much more specific and penetrating concept. The Gospel is that element in the Christian religion which is not subject to compromise, adaptation, or temporizing. It is simply there, to be accepted or rejected.

In *St. Luke 20:17*, Jesus quotes Psalm 118: "The very stone which the builders rejected has become the head of the corner," and adds, "Everyone who falls on that stone will be broken in pieces; but when it falls on anyone it will crush him."

The word "Gospel" means, of course, "good news." What is good news for one person may be bad news for somebody else. But if the news is authentic, you cannot revise it to fit your desires or plans or wishes. You just have to adapt yourself to it. When the Gospel is made known to us, we cannot argue with it. We can only use it as the cornerstone of our lives, or run the risk of breaking our heads or our legs on it. It is there, period.

Toward the end of the nineteenth century people made a resolute effort to find in the New Testament the evidence of a "historical Jesus"—the real Jesus—who would validate the religious concepts of the nineteenth century when all the distortions and misinterpretations of His fallible followers in their fallible writings were cleared away.

This was a time of great optimism and confidence in human progress. It was a period of faith in science and the universal validity of natural law. It was also a time of scorn toward the crude concepts of the "pre-scientific" ages of the past. These preconceptions required the Jesus of the nineteenth century to be one who did not preach the imminent end of the world, who did not believe in devils, who did not concern Himself with the supernatural in religion in any vital way, but called upon men to be brothers, to be good, and to work for a better world. This "simple religion of Jesus" was, according to some Christian thinkers, to be found in the New Testament hidden beneath the "religion about Christ" which had been foisted on the Church by someone—probably St. Paul. The product of this kind of thinking was a "social gospel" which turned out to be much more social than gospel.

In more recent years it has been recognized that the effort to "modernize Jesus" rests upon no foundation whatever. As a man, he was certainly not a nineteenth-century man—nor a twentieth-century man, either. "The quest of the historical Jesus" has ended at an impenetrable barrier. Nothing is known about Him historically except the effect He had upon a group of unimportant and mostly uneducated people in a corner of the world nearly 2,000 years ago.

There isn't any history or biography of Jesus. There is only a series of intensely partisan pamphlets by people who were trying to show that He was the Christ. If their bias is refined out of the picture, it isn't long before nothing is left. If there is any Gospel at all, it is the bias of the New Testament writers themselves—the thing they were trying to prove, to understand, to follow, and to proclaim among their contemporaries.

The Gospels and the Epistles of the New Testament represent the Church's testimony that Jesus is the Christ. The effort to go behind the Gospel record has resulted not in finding Jesus directly but in finding the Church.

The Church said that the Holy Spirit bore witness with it to the good news of Jesus Christ—that the Spirit confirmed the apostles' word "with signs following"; that He inspired prophets and evangelists; that He strengthened and guided and enlightened them. The First Epistle of John asserts: "The Spirit is the witness, because the Spirit is the truth." In our day the Spirit has once again become the central figure in the *dramatis personae* of early Christianity. We know no more about Jesus than we know about the Holy Ghost. Indeed, all we know of Jesus we know through the Holy Ghost.

Christ promised His disciples that the Holy Spirit

would "lead you into all truth." Yet the primary activity of the Holy Spirit in the Church is not to bring forth new truth, but to bear witness to the Good News which was the same in 60 A.D. as in 1960 A.D. The Gospel is there. The Church must adapt to it as well as the world.

The varied crises our civilization faces—religious, philosophical, political, and social—give our troubled time a kinship with the world of religious, philosophical, political, and social turmoil in which the Gospel was first proclaimed. "If you're not confused, you just don't understand the situation," could have been said in the first century, and it is the intellectual rallying cry of the twentieth.

The Gospel speaks meaningfully to a time of crisis because it is about a crisis. The Christian announcement that "the end of all things is at hand" is a reasonable forecast in our day, whether or not you believe anything else that Christianity says. Even though fallen man has lost the faculty of knowing his heavenly destination, he knows very well that he is not going to be here forever, either individually or as a race.

O God, whose blessed Son was manifested that he might destroy the works of the devil, and make us the sons of God, and heirs of eternal life; Grant us, we beseech thee, that, having this hope, we may purify ourselves, even as he is pure; that, when he shall appear again with power and great glory, we may be made like unto him in his eternal and glorious kingdom; where with thee, O Father, and thee, O Holy Ghost, he liveth and reigneth ever, one God, world without end. Amen.

Book of Common Prayer, page 117

* * * * *

The fact that human history will have an end is just as true in one period as in another. But this is one of the periods when this fact is borne in upon everybody's mind. Are we only an episode in the universe, a lost cause along with the trilobites and the dinosaurs? Or is the meaning of our lives something beyond history, beyond chemistry and physics, beyond the entire order of nature? What about God? Does He exist? What place do we have in His creation? What place do I have?

The Gospel is the answer to questions like these. It is not a philosophical or theoretical answer. It is a factual answer, a piece of good news. "So you are worrying about these questions? Well, let me tell you about something that happened that throws an altogether different light on the situation."

In ancient Babylon, the Jews languished as a captive people, torn from their homes to do forced labor in a strange land with no reasonable prospect of deliverance. What hope did they have? "How shall we sing the Lord's song in a strange land?" But those who remembered their nation's past knew something that threw an altogether different light on the situation. They remembered their bondage in Egypt. They remembered how the Lord had taken pity on them and had led them up out of Egypt with a mighty arm; how He had miraculously rescued them from all the power of the Egyptian army at the Red Sea. Because of God's mighty acts in the past, they knew something about God and about themselves and their relation to Him. The good news of this deliverance was annually recalled at the feast of the Passover with a re-enactment of the meal which the Israelites hastily prepared, in accordance with Moses' instructions, as they made ready to depart. It was the subject of songs and stories, and it was the foundation of prophecies of deliverance from today's vicissitudes. It was the thing that held the nation together in Babylonian exile and it was the dynamic force that eventually brought about the return to the Promised Land.

In twentieth-century America, the parish is the focal point of an equally vivid recollection of redemption and an equally confident promise of deliverance. But the Gospel of Jesus Christ is far vaster in scope. The issue is not the fate of one nation concerned about its territory, prosperity, and longevity, but the fate of all mankind forever. The ultimate arena of action is not even confined to this earth, but covers the whole created universe. The God whose redemptive purpose is revealed in Jesus Christ is the maker of heaven and earth, and of all things visible and invisible.

Searching for a metaphor to express the magnitude of what is happening, St. Paul says it is as if the whole creation were giving birth to a baby. (*Romans* 8:22.) "And not only the creation, but we ourselves, who have the first fruits of the Spirit, groan inwardly as we wait for adoption as sons, the redemption of our bodies."

When Jesus was taken away to be crucified, He fulfilled for all future generations the crisis of relationship to God that confronted the children of Israel at the Red Sea. He was mankind bearing the burden of man's sins, the weight of mortality, and the silence of the universe at man's inhumanity to man. In His Resurrection and Ascension, He passed through a Red Sea that belongs not just to the history of Israel but to the history of all men everywhere; and He came out victorious on the other side.

The Easter hymns of the Church never tire of drawing parallels between Israel's deliverance at the Red Sea and Christ's Resurrection.

> The day of resurrection!
> Earth, tell it out abroad;
> The Passover of gladness,
> The Passover of God.
> From death to life eternal,
> From earth unto the sky,
> Our Christ hath brought us over
> With hymns of victory.

And the parish church is also the focal point of the passover meal which, like the ancient Jewish passover, is a recollection of redemption and a promise of future deliverance. "Do this in remembrance of me," said Jesus: "This is the new covenant in my blood." "For as often as you eat this bread and drink this cup," said St. Paul, "you proclaim the Lord's death until he comes."

Central in the Jewish passover was the lamb which was killed and eaten on the last day of the feast. The Book of Exodus relates the events of the first passover, when the blood of the lamb on the doorposts of the Israelites' houses served as a sign that the destroying angel was to pass over those houses. "You shall observe this rite as an ordinance for you and for your sons forever," said Moses. "And when your children say to you, 'What do you mean by this service?' you shall say, 'It is the sacrifice of the Lord's passover, for he passed over the houses of the people of Israel in Egypt, when he slew the Egyptians but spared our houses.' "

The Holy Communion in the parish church of today centers upon the "Lamb of God that taketh away the sins of the world," who is both priest and victim in the Christian passover. In the words of the Prayer Book preface for Easter, "He is the very Paschal Lamb, which was offered for us, and hath taken away the sin of the world; who by his death hath destroyed death, and by his rising to life again hath restored to us everlasting life."

In a very real sense, the parish celebration of the Holy Communion—the Eucharist—*is* the Gospel. Here, the good news of redemption finds its fullest and deepest earthly expression. It is the passover of the New Covenant, a "contract" of God, not just with one nation, but with all men who will respond to His offer of Salvation; a participation in the body and blood of Him who by his death has destroyed death and by his Resurrection has won for us everlasting life.

Almighty God, whose compassions fail not, and whose loving-kindness reacheth unto the world's end; We give thee humble thanks for opening heathen lands to the light of thy truth; for making paths in the deep waters and highways in the desert; and for planting thy Church in all the earth. Grant, we beseech thee, unto us thy servants, that with lively faith we may labour abundantly to make known to all men thy blessed gift of eternal life; through Jesus Christ our Lord. Amen.

Book of Common Prayer, page 38

There is a certain inversion of emphasis in a great deal of present-day thinking about the Gospel. We tend to think of Christianity as primarily a process that is going on within our own minds and souls. This process is, of course, an authentic and essential part of Christianity. We must learn the faith, believe it, and order our lives in accordance with it. Yet, the first and most important point about the Gospel is its objectivity, its "isness," its historical character.

Whether or not we believe in it, it has happened. Whether or not it is our victory, it is God's victory. When the United States and its allies won World War II, the fact of victory had many implications for individuals. Everybody had to learn the fact first, then believe it, and make plans for ordering his life in the light of this earth-shaking fact.

A man who made his living by manufacturing ammunition might be glad or sorry that the war had ended, depending upon what values were uppermost in his life. The one thing that he certainly had to do in either case was to recognize that the war had ended.

To think of the Holy Communion in terms of this factual, historical character of the Gospel may bring us closer to the meaning attached to the Lord's Supper by the early Church. The service was being regularly and faithfully celebrated by the Church long before there was any precise explanation of what good it did to the people who took part in it. St. Paul and St. John give a good deal of Eucharistic doctrine in their writings in rather general terms, but hardly in such terms as to satisfy the curiosity of later centuries as to the specific effects upon or benefits gained by the individual recipient.

Over the centuries, theologians and laypeople alike have tried to pin down in precise language just what takes place when the Church celebrates Holy Communion. Controversy has centered primarily on the nature of Christ's Eucharistic presence and on the effects of the sacrament on the recipient.

In the course of all the controversy, one thing has been universally agreed: that the service is, among other things, a memorial, a remembrance. This, after all, was what Jesus Himself stressed in instituting the Sacrament: "Do this in remembrance of me." But it is questionable whether European man—especially modern European or American man—understands the dynamic significance of this act of remembrance in the minds of the Jewish world in which the Church was born.

History and the remembrance of God's past redemptive actions among His people were not mere intellectual pursuits to the people of Israel. They were the very stuff of daily life. As Arnold Toynbee has said, the great contribution of the Hebrew prophets to the thought of the world was an "interpretation of history." God is revealed in history, His will is made known in history, our present relationship to Him is the fruit of our past history, of His promises to our fathers, of our failures to meet His demands. Triumph and defeat, judgment and redemption, represent the impact of the past upon the present and future. The modern American tends to regard the past as dead and the future as problematical. But to the Jewish mind, the past was anything but dead and the future was in the hands of a God who made promises and kept them.

In the Holy Communion something happens "here

and now"—in the present. But the thing that happens is that here and now we enter into the redemptive events that happened long ago and become a part of them. We become one with Peter and James and John in the remembrance of their Lord, and in their proclamation of the Gospel to the world. We become one not only with His disciples but with Christ Himself in the redemption which He wrought for us. What was "history" becomes "our history." What was "the past" becomes "our past." What was Jesus' life becomes "our life."

A naturalized American has the same founding fathers as one who was born an American. His ancestors tamed the West; his side won the nation's wars, whether or not his ancestors after the flesh happened to be on the other side. So we, as adoptive sons of God in Baptism, become in Holy Communion one body and one blood with God the Son in a "remembrance" made complete by His sacramental presence under the forms of bread and wine. "We become," as Dom Gregory Dix has put it, "what we are."

To the newly baptized in a time of persecution, St. Peter's First Epistle described the status of those who had been "born anew, not of perishable seed but imperishable, through the living and abiding word of God"; "You are a chosen race, a royal priesthood, a holy nation, God's own people, that you may declare the wonderful deeds of him who called you out of darkness into his marvelous light. Once you were no people but now you are God's people; once you had not received mercy but now you have received mercy."

Entry into this "chosen race," this "royal priesthood," this "holy nation" involves a relationship not only to God's mighty acts in the past, but also to its future destiny. The Gospel itself is concerned with both past and future, seeing the one as the ground of the other.

Almighty and everliving God, we most heartily thank thee, for that thou dost vouchsafe to feed us who have duly received these holy mysteries, with the spiritual food of the most precious Body and Blood of thy Son our Saviour Jesus Christ; and dost assure us thereby of thy favour and goodness towards us; and that we are very members incorporate in the mystical body of thy Son, which is the blessed company of all faithful people; and are also heirs through hope of thy everlasting kingdom, by the merits of his most precious death and passion. And we humbly beseech thee, O heavenly Father, so to assist us with thy grace, that we may continue in that holy fellowship, and do all such good works as thou hast prepared for us to walk in; through Jesus Christ our Lord, to whom, with thee and the Holy Ghost, be all honour and glory, world without end. Amen.

Book of Common Prayer, page 83

❋ ❋ 5 ❋ ❋

Rediscovering Eschatology

THE FIRST GENERATION of Christians lived in the imminent expectation of the end of the world. They believed themselves to be as close to the Second Coming of Christ in His glorious majesty to judge the living and the dead as they were to the events of the recent past whereby He had opened up for them a way to reconciliation with God. The Jewish prophets had asserted that history was not a mere matter of chance, of material cause and effect, nor of endless cycles, but rather a divinely governed movement toward a divinely established goal. John the Baptist had announced that the time was filled up, the kingdom of heaven was at hand, judgment day was just around the corner. And Jesus had come and shown, both by word and by deed, that He was the Saviour and Judge and King whom God had sent to complete the story of mankind.

Almost two thousand years have gone by since the end of all things was announced to be at hand, but the end has not arrived. From time to time in the intervening centuries, individuals and groups have decided on various grounds that judgment day was about to take place and have made preparations that ended in anti-climax. People have settled their affairs, sold their possessions, and gathered together for prayer, fasting, and exhortation, only to disband when the period of waiting became so long that they had to give up.

Some religions may be oblivious of the world, but Christianity is not. It is an assertion about history, it lives in history, and if history does not proceed as expected, its failure to do so has theological and spiritual implications.

The area of Christian thought that deals with Christ's Second Coming, judgment day, heaven, and hell, is called *eschatology*. The term is derived from a Greek word meaning "the study of the last things." What a person believes about the last things is influenced not only by his ideas about God but also by his ideas about geology, astronomy, physics, chemistry, and biology. Scientific facts are as intractable as the facts of the Gospel. And the individual who has clothed his concept of the Gospel in scientific theories which do not square with presently known facts is in real trouble.

Thus, in every age, the preaching of the Gospel faces a dilemma. Unless it is an assertion about God's redemptive acts in the world of space and time, of sight and sense, it is not the Gospel. But if it clings stubbornly to outmoded concepts of the world of space and time, it becomes an outmoded Gospel.

When the Lord's Prayer was first said, it was a prayer about the end of the world—an eschatological prayer. It was the motto of a group of revolutionaries awaiting an overturn in the established order of things. Jesus taught this prayer to His disciples in response to their request, "Lord, teach us to pray." When they asked him for instruction about praying, they were not beginning from scratch, as it were; they were loyal sons of Israel who had been praying all their lives in synagogue and temple and at home. What they were asking for was a form of prayer that would embody the new teaching about the kindgom of God which Jesus had been giving them. How do you pray in these last days when you are waiting for the kingdom of God to come with power?

This background colors every petition—for the coming of the kingdom, for our daily bread in the meantime, for forgiveness, and for deliverance from temptation and the power of the devil. To modern Christians, the word "temptation" usually means the attractive power of our selfish desires. But to those who first said the Lord's Prayer it referred to the fiery trials of persecution and tribulation which would take place before the end.

Similarly, the ethical principles, the acts of mercy, the form of organization, the entire ethos of the Church in its first days, were shaped by its urgent expectation of the Second Coming.

But within the period in which the New Testament was written, it was already becoming clear to the disciples that the world was likely to continue for a good while longer. The Christian layman had to keep at his daily work, earn his own living, get married, have children, plan for their earthly as well as their heavenly future. He couldn't just sit around waiting for the end. And while this might have a disillusioning effect on some aspects of what the first Christians had thought the Gospel meant, it opened up far wider possibilities for the preaching of the Gospel to the whole world.

Actually, by the end of the first century, the fundamental problem of the Church's eschatological emphasis had been met. If Christianity had to wait a hundred years for the Second Coming, the problem was basically the same as if the waiting period were a thousand, or five thousand, years. An interim which is likely to cover the lifetime of everybody now living requires an understanding of the Gospel which makes it relevant to life in this world as well as to life in the world to come.

Christianity had proclaimed from the start a vigorous belief in the resurrection of the dead. The fact that there would be many generations of Christians to be raised on judgment day was not too difficult to accept. The declaration which later became a part of the Apostles' Creed —"And he shall come again, with glory, to judge both the quick and the dead"—meant much the same thing to the Church at the end of the first century as it does today.

Almighty God, give us grace that we may cast away the works of darkness, and put upon us the armour of light, now in the time of this mortal life, in which thy Son Jesus Christ came to visit us in great humility; that in the last day, when he shall come again in his glorious majesty to judge both the quick and the dead, we may rise to the life immortal, through him who liveth and reigneth with thee and the Holy Ghost, now and ever. Amen.

Book of Common Prayer, page 90

✻ ✻ ✻ ✻ ✻

When St. Paul exhorted the Romans to "cast off the works of darkness and put on the armour of light," he did so on the assumption that "the night is far spent, the day is at hand." He was saying, "get dressed up for the day of judgment." His advice is still good, even though we now reinterpret it to apply to our clothing for "this mortal life." For one thing, the day of judgment is in a real sense always at hand. For another thing, if we have become members of Christ, participants in His life, we are already "in the day," living in the kingdom even though we are surrounded by a world which does not know it.

Such reinterpretation of biblical truths to fit into a changed world-view is sometimes called "demythologizing" and "remythologizing" by present-day theologians. Mankind's earlier efforts to explain history, natural forces, and the origins and ends of things took the form of stories or "myths" in which a human or animal hero was the protagonist. The mythology of an ancient culture summed up its world-view, and in this sense it is true that the Gospel was first proclaimed and has been later understood in terms of the different mythologies or world-views, of different times and places.

In primitive cultures a myth is not looked upon as symbolic fiction. It is a serious account, in terms of the facts and scientific laws available to that culture, of why the sun rises, how fire was discovered, what causes the cycle of the seasons. Accordingly, as theologians use the word "mythology" today, it is applied to the serious attempts of more sophisticated societies to explain natural phenomena and spiritual forces. The belief that the world was flat with a heaven above it and a hell beneath it belonged to the mythology of one period in history in this extended sense of the word "mythology." Obviously a Christian who believed in this kind of universe would enshrine his faith in language which needs restatement for a Christian who believes in a different kind of universe.

To apply such terms as "demythologizing" and "remythologizing" to the Christian faith may seem to imply that the Gospel itself is mythology. But this is not the case. The rising and setting of the sun, the progression of the seasons, are not mythology; they are the things which mythology tries to explain. Similarly, the Gospel is not mythology, but it is something which mythology tries to explain.

In a scientific age, the language of mythology is impersonal, scientific. Human and animal heroes are replaced by natural forces and laws. Recent centuries have seen extensive efforts to explain Jesus and the Gospel, and all things human and divine, in terms of this scientific mythology, which has been notably successful up to a point in explaining such things as the behavior of the solar system and the heredity of plants and animals.

The "social gospel" with its "simple religion of Jesus" was a mythologizing of the Gospel to fit in with the perpetual motion machine of the Newtonian universe. Sir Isaac Newton, who formulated some of the basic laws of that materialistic universe, was not a materialist himself. Among his other claims to distinction, he was a theologian of no little merit, with a lively belief in the supernatural.

In our own day, the mechanistic, closed-system universe of Newtonian physics no longer serves as an adequate explanation even for physical phenomena. The universe of Einstein is an altogether different kind of place. Ironically enough, Albert Einstein expressed in his writings on religious subjects a mechanistic idea of God which fitted the outmoded physical concepts he had helped to destroy. If Newton was blissfully unaware of the discrepancies between his religion and his physics, so was his great successor.

There was not much room for eschatology in an eternally existing universe composed of indestructible matter operating according to immutable laws which could theoretically predict the exact position and velocity of everything in the world a million years hence. For many years, eschatological preaching and eschatological thinking have been largely a monopoly of minority groups of Christians who were strong in the knowledge of the Bible but weak in their knowledge of most other things. Though the Church maintained its faith in the Second Coming, the Last Judgment, heaven, and hell, it did not talk about these things very much.

Today, however, eschatology is being rediscovered. The "mythology"—*i.e.*, the scientific world-view—of today is no longer in open conflict with the fundamental assumptions of Christianity about the origin and destiny of man. In fact, it is no longer quite respectable to have a cosmology ("science of everything") based exclusively upon the data of natural science. Mastery of the principles of atomic energy seems to most of us to be a curse as much as a blessing, because the question of who will employ these principles, and where and how, is an urgently important matter on which natural science can give no guidance. We have discovered that the world of men can come to an end in some other way than by a geological or astronomic calamity, and the imaginable manner of its ending bears some noteworthy resemblances to the "mythology" used to describe the "end of the age" in the Bible.

Those who go their way unaware of the critical nature of our times are well epitomized in Jesus' comment: "As the days of Noah were, so shall also the coming of the Son of man be. They were eating and drinking, marrying and giving in marriage, until the day that Noah entered the ark . . . until the flood came, and took them all away."

The Gospel of a humanistic Jesus spreading moral uplift in a world which needed only educational and scientific and material progress has been rudely demythologized by the events of recent history. That Gospel had a mythology of a kingdom of God on earth attained by the efforts of men of good will; it directed its warnings of divine judgment and damnation toward those who stood in the way of progress.

Something better is needed—something that recognizes the strong likelihood that man will defeat himself on the battleground of history, something that consecrates the present moment as an opportunity for human dignity and significance even though the next moment may be the end of everything. Something is needed that recognizes the desire for a better world which we believe is divinely implanted in us, but does not tell us to place our hope in the fragile houses of cards that seem to be our best efforts toward the building of such a world. Something is needed to bridge the gap between the concept of a just and loving God and the fact of undeserved and unavoidable suffering. Something is needed to overcome the fact that in national policy as in the home, in business as in our fraternal and charitable associations, the good that we would we do not: but the evil which we would not, that we do.

Our age is asking the right questions about the ultimate ends of life.

O Lord, raise up, we pray thee, thy power, and come among us, and with great might succour us; that whereas, through our sins and wickedness, we are sore let and hindered in running the race that is set before us, thy bountiful grace and mercy may speedily help and deliver us; through Jesus Christ our Lord, to whom, with thee and the Holy Ghost, be honour and glory world without end. Amen.

Book of Common Prayer, page 95

* * * * *

The general body of human knowledge today has no answer to the question whether democracy or communism will triumph, or whether each will destroy the other leaving the world to the kissing bug and the speedwell weed (which happen to be so constructed that they are specially well fitted to withstand atomic radiation). Nor does the general body of human knowledge point with an unerring finger toward a spiritual interpretation of the universe or a vindication of the eschatological views of the first Christians.

It cannot even be said that Christian thinkers are in a position to advance a unified, well-worked-out cosmology that gives a convincing description of how the world began and how it will end. They cannot say where heaven or hell is located. They cannot imagine the conditions under which the Son of man will return or the Last Judgment take place.

If a "remythologizing" of eschatology for today involves the vivid pictorial images that characterized prescientific descriptions, then eschatology still awaits a meaningful remythologizing.

And yet, the present-day Christian finds himself moving with renewed confidence among the eschatological symbols and images of the New Testament. If these passages ever did purport to be a literal description of the end of the world, they certainly are not so regarded today. They are descriptions of the indescribable, explanations of the unexplainable, imaginings of the unimaginable. Nevertheless, they are faithful and honest projections of the deepest religious insights the world has ever had or ever will have.

Preaching to the Athenians, St. Paul is recorded in the Book of Acts as saying that God "has fixed a day on which he will judge the world in righteousness by a man whom he has appointed, and of this he has given assurance to all men by raising him from the dead."

The Gospel speaks with entire confidence about the unimaginable future because its confidence is rooted in a fact of history—the fact of Jesus of Nazareth. The Jews in Babylon spoke confidently of their national future because their confidence was rooted in the facts of their past history. God had done the impossible before, and it was more reasonable than not to expect Him to do it again. They were not counting on the reliability of nature, but on the reliability of God.

Similarly, the Christian hope about the ultimate end of human striving is not based upon the probabilities of science but upon the certainty of divine redemption.

The "how" and the "when" and "where" are matters of interest. Christians combine what they know of Christ with what they know of natural laws and of human affairs to create a Christian cosmology for our times. But it is strictly a provisional cosmology which can be corrected or abandoned if circumstances so demand. It is not hard to conceive of a fourth-dimensional location for heaven, nor to think of a resurrection body in terms of its basic principles of organization rather than its material constituents (which are constantly changing, anyhow). But such speculations are hardly held with enough firmness to earn the name of a "mythology." The myths that are still powerful today are those of nineteenth-century science, widely believed among the general public just as the common folk of ancient Greece held on to their sprightly gods and goddesses long after most thinking men had abandoned them.

The "why" and "whether" of the ultimate closing of the book of history are another matter. When you see the flour and the baking powder and the sugar and the apples and the pans and the other appurtenances of pie-making spread out in the kitchen, you know that a pie is going to be baked, though you may not know how or when or, perhaps even where. We see in the coming of God the Son to earth, His life, His death, His resurrection and ascension, in the coming of the Holy Ghost and the establishment of the Church, the preparations for the event toward which the whole creation has been moving. Said Jesus: "When you see a cloud rising in the west, you say at once, 'A shower is coming'; and it so happens. And when you see the south wind blowing, you say, 'There will be scorching heat'; and it happens. You hypocrites! You know how to interpret the appearance of earth and sky; but why do you not know how to interpret the present time?"

Though we cannot sit down to the table and wait for the pie to be served, though we resent and reject the idea that a promise of "pie in the sky" is a sufficient answer to the woes of this world, we know that the eschatological element is as central to our Christian faith as the baking of the pie is to all the preparations for doing so. We would be missing the whole point of the Gospel if we thought that Christianity was merely a prescription for a more abundant life in this world.

O God, the protector of all that trust in thee, without whom nothing is strong, nothing is holy; Increase and multiply upon us thy mercy; that, thou being our ruler and guide, we may so pass through things temporal, that we finally lose not the things eternal. Grant this, O heavenly Father, for the sake of Jesus Christ our Lord. Amen.

Book of Common Prayer, page 194

The belief, in the words of the Epistle to the Hebrews, that "we have here no lasting city, but we seek the city which is to come," necessarily has a profound influence on the attitude of the Christian toward this present world. From time to time, over the course of history, Christian groups have taken an "extricationist" point of view. They have regarded the task of the Church as to save people from a lost and dying world and have felt that the Church ought not to concern itself with great social, economic, and political problems.

It is one thing for a poor and powerless Christian to be an extricationist, but it is a somewhat different thing for an influential and powerful Christian to assert that the Church ought to leave the world alone. The one is confessing that he cannot do much to the world; the other is guarding his own area of worldly power and influence from the inroads of the Gospel. A few generations ago, it seemed that some of the most vigorous advocates for an otherworldly form of Christianity were people who in their daily occupations were the most vigorous practitioners of a this-worldly way of life.

"Pie in the sky" was a popular song of the earlier and more radical days of the labor movement. It lampooned the submissive attitude toward the world's evils and injustices that seemed to characterize the presentation of the Gospel in nineteenth-century America. If the "social gospel" was too much "social" and not enough "gospel," the more conservative and standard form of Christianity in those days was not social enough to be Gospel.

When the eschatological, otherworldly side of the Gospel becomes an excuse for retreating from the opportunities and obligations of this world, the Gospel is being distorted as grievously as it is when the otherworldly side is neglected.

The Gospel is, as was previously stated, an assertion about history. In pointing toward a supernatural destiny for man, a divine winding up of human affairs, it does not render history meaningless. On the contrary, the

Gospel gives history a meaning that applies urgently and immediately to everything that happens in this world.

The Christian who is a participant in business, politics, and community living cannot divide himself in two and be a Christian in church and a secularist everywhere else. The Gospel is concerned with the whole of man, not just with an isolated area of life that carries the label "spiritual."

Oppression, violence, injustice, hunger, and suffering are more, rather than less, intolerable when they are looked upon in the light of the divine destiny revealed to us by Jesus Christ. "Woe unto the world because of offences!" He said. "For it must needs be that offences come; but woe to that man by whom the offence cometh!" Wherever we have failed to speak or act against man's inhumanity to man, our failure is an offence against God Himself.

Life in this world is not unimportant. It is crucially important. And, while mankind's affairs proceed toward a final judgment, particular judgments take place again and again upon individuals and groups and nations and civilizations that have tried to find for themselves a permanent stopping place on the road to the kingdom of God. It seems that the divine judgment falls equally upon the wicked and the not-so-bad. Like the lost homing pigeons, we have subjected ourselves to futility and disaster not primarily because of what we have done but because of what we have not done. We have failed to seek first the kingdom of God and His righteousness, and have made our spiritual homes in a place that is not home.

The Christian working for the betterment of his community or the world often finds that he can accomplish most by allying himself with others in political and economic groupings that have similar objectives. And sometimes these groups pursue their goals with such drive and effectiveness that they seem to be doing more for mankind than the Church itself. In the field of racial desegregation, for example, local congregations often move in such a timid and gingerly manner that the Church is sometimes charged with being the last stronghold of segregation.

The Church is not exempt from the judgment of God. A racialist Church has abandoned the Gospel and will in turn be abandoned by the Lord of the Gospel. Yet, the Church has seen many great secular movements come and go and has continued through all of them to bear witness to an even deeper and more radical revolution—a revolution which never seems to be timely because it is timeless.

In most of the great forward steps taken by civilization in the past five hundred years, the forces of Christianity have appeared to be reluctant, if not hostile—in the renaissance, the rise of democracy, the industrial revolution, the labor movement, and now the extension of the benefits of these things to people of all races. Yet, it is a peculiarity of all these developments that they occurred in Christian countries. In considerable measure, they represent the ministry of the laity, exercised outside the walls of the Church, even outside the formal context of the Church, but yet bringing some reflection of the Good News of Christ to contemporary men and women.

In a sense, the Christian demand that all things be viewed from the standpoint of eternity sets up a standard of evaluation that is not too remote but too immediate for practical effectiveness in secular affairs. When St. Paul sent the slave Onesimus back to his master Philemon, he did not speak out against the institution of slavery. What he did speak about was the brotherhood that ought to exist between slave and master. "Perhaps this is why he was parted from you for a while [he had run away], that you might have him back forever, no longer as a slave but more than a slave, as a beloved brother . . ." Social movements live by tomorrow, and are willing to coerce and destroy and despise and pillage and burn for the hope of that better tomorrow. But tomorrow is always one day too late for those who live under the shadow of judgment day.

Christianity maintains, more or less permanently, an ambivalent attitude toward great movements for human betterment, and the Christian who takes part in such a movement must do the same. The kingdom of God has not been and will not be brought in by the expansion of learning, the extension of democracy, the increase of available goods and services, the economic betterment of working people, or the tearing down of racial barriers. Yet each of these things in its day represents an opening of the eyes to the blind, release to the captives, liberty to the oppressed, good news to the poor. They have the character of the "signs of the Gospel," the paradigmatic actions that made it possible for men to recognize the Messiah when He came down to earth and walked among them.

When, however, such movements claim to be "some great cause, God's new Messiah," in the words of James Russell Lowell's heretical hymn, then we realize that what we are witnessing is a fight among the homeless pigeons of the city streets, a struggle that is relevant not to their heavenly destination but rather to their aimless and compromised condition. What they are sharing is not the fruits of human victory but the crusts of human defeat.

For the Christian finds the meaning of history, and the goal of all movements within history, finally and completely only in the unimaginable future event when a great multitude which no man can number of all nations and kindreds and peoples and tribes and tongues shall stand before the throne and before the Lamb, crying, "Salvation to our God . . . and unto the Lamb." "They shall hunger no more, neither thirst any more; neither shall the sun light on them, nor any heat. For the Lamb which is in the midst of the throne shall feed them, and shall lead them unto living fountains of waters: and God shall wipe away all tears from their eyes."

Almighty God, who hast created man in thine own image; Grant us grace fearlessly to contend against evil, and to make no peace with oppression; and, that we may reverently use our freedom, help us to employ it in the maintenance of justice among men and nations, to the glory of thy holy Name; through Jesus Christ our Lord. Amen.

Book of Common Prayer, page 44

The vision of the consummation of all things in The Revelation of St. John the Divine figures forth an event that finally and completely reveals the meaning of history. And yet, we can well imagine that the philosophers and scientists and theologians and other inquisitive people among the saints will wish to ask God one further question.

"We understand the goal well enough," they might say. "But why all the long process beforehand? Why was man placed on earth and led through all his struggles and vicissitudes for all those millions of years?"

To which God might reply: "You were supposed to enjoy it."

If homing man had not originally lost his way, he still would have had a long and at times wearisome journey to his heavenly destination. Very likely he would have been beset by lions and tigers, by the measles, by cold weather and hot, by shortages of food and clothing. Yet, even fallen man, who multiplies his troubles a thousandfold by being his own worst enemy, will testify in most times and places that life on earth is a pretty good thing.

The game *is* worth the candle. This simple fact is a fundamental part of the data of religion, although somehow it can easily be lost from sight in theological discussions. God does not owe us any apology for having given us an opportunity to play the game of living.

We, with the other animals, are fulfilling the divine purpose when we are simply engaged in the work of being creatures—of eating and sleeping and raising our young and building our homes and gathering our supplies. We are fulfilling the divine purpose when we simply sit back and rest and enjoy the world that God has made. So important was this aspect of religion to the Jewish Church that it was enshrined in the Ten Commandments. "Remember that thou keep holy the Sabbath-day. . . ."

The Christian needs no further justification for eating and drinking and making merry than that he is one of God's creatures in God's world. In fact, an act of praise to God for His creation was a prominent feature of the early liturgies of the Christian Church.

The Gospel gives natural man a supernatural frame of reference in a kingdom that is yet to come. But, paradoxically, the kingdom of God is right here, right now—"in the midst of you" or "inside of you," as Jesus told the Pharisees in St. Luke 17:21.

The kingdom of God exists wherever the rule of the heavenly King is acknowledged. The kingdom of God is encountered wherever Jesus is encountered. "If it is by the Spirit of God that I cast out demons," said Jesus, "then the kingdom of God has come upon you."

Accordingly, the daily round of work and play and rest, the concerns of home and job and family, of social life and amusements, of politics, of waging war and making peace—all these things are things that take place within the context of the kingdom of God. Each one of them is something that may have to be given up for the sake of Jesus and the Gospel. Each of them is something which we rediscover within the framework of Jesus and the Gospel.

"Verily I say unto you, There is no man that hath left house, or brethren, or sisters, or father, or mother, or wife, or children, or lands, for my sake and the gospel's, but he shall receive an hundredfold now in this time, houses, and brethren, and sisters, and mothers, and children, and lands, with persecutions; and in the world to come eternal life."

This was the comment of Jesus when the rich young man "went away sorrowful" because he could not bring himself to give up his possessions for Christ. There is nothing unchristian about having and enjoying this world's goods; but our attachment to them must be made subordinate to our loyalty to Christ. Under his loving rule, we shall receive a hundredfold—and in this world—what we had before, together with the persecutions that come from our commitment to Him. But first, we have to be able to give up anything that constitutes a challenge to His kingship over our hearts.

We give Thee thanks, Holy Father, for Thy holy name, which Thou hast made to tabernacle in our hearts, and for the knowledge and faith and immortality which Thou hast made known unto us through Thy Son Jesus; Thine is the glory for ever and ever. Thou, Almighty Master, didst create all things for Thy name's sake and didst give food and drink unto men for enjoyment, that they might render thanks unto Thee; but didst bestow on us spiritual food and drink and eternal life through Thy Son. Before all things we give Thee thanks that Thou are powerful; Thine is the glory for ever and ever. Remember Lord, Thy Church, to deliver it from all evil and to perfect it in Thy love; and gather it together from the four winds—even the Church which has been sanctified—into Thy kingdom which Thou hast prepared for it; For Thine is the power and the glory for ever and ever. May grace come and may this world pass away. Hosanna to the God of David. If any man is holy, let him come; if any man is not, let him repent. Maran atha [*Lord, come*]. Amen. [From *The Didache,* or *Teaching of the Apostles,* a very ancient book of Church order. Lightfoot's translation]

❋ ❋ 6 ❋ ❋

Activism and Action

IF THERE IS any one passage of the New Testament against which the modern American rebels, it is the story of Martha and Mary.

"A woman named Martha received Jesus into her house. And she had a sister called Mary, who sat at the Lord's feet and listened to his teaching. But Martha was distracted with much serving; and she went to him and said, 'Lord, do you not care that my sister has left me to serve alone? Tell her then to help me.' But the Lord answered her, 'Martha, Martha, you are anxious and troubled about many things; one thing is needful. Mary has chosen the good portion, which shall not be taken away from her.' " (*St. Luke 10:38-42*)

But, in spite of what the Lord said about it, St. Martha is the patron saint of the American housewife—and of the American businessman, too. The idea is firmly fixed in our minds that it is better to be busy on behalf of the Lord than to listen to Him. Under these conditions, it is not surprising that the local church in modern America should tend to become a place where people are busy on behalf of the Lord instead of sitting at His feet and listening.

Perhaps the variety and profusion of parish activities in today's world is to some extent a reasonable and necessary mythologizing of the Gospel so that it may be understood and accepted by our civilization. If the modern American believes something to be important, he must build a handsome building for it, hold meetings about it, give money to it, solicit members for it, and in all ways make it the biggest and best and liveliest thing he knows.

But the Gospel is something else. "One thing is needful." Only one course needs to be served at the Lord's supper, and it is the only parish supper that is necessary. All the rest is a concession to the quaint folkways of the tribes that currently inhabit our continent.

The Church in modern America cannot make contact with the minds of ordinary men and women through the dramatic world-renouncing monasticism of the ancient monks in the Egyptian desert. Nor can the Gospel be made known in our times through the complex feudal structures, magnificence, and power that made sense to medieval man. This is the day of the committee and the volunteer worker. Unless Christ can be encountered at the round table or in the money-raising campaign, the modern American might never come across Him at all.

So, the well-organized parish, offering a full round of activities to its people, may well be a parish that is preaching the Gospel effectively in our times. The thing that was wrong with Martha was not that she had undertaken to make a large social event out of our Lord's visit. The thing that was wrong was that she had driven herself to distraction with her ambitious project and now demanded that her sister fall into the same frantic condition.

Such a communion in anxiety is often demanded in parish life today. A wholesome activity swells up and ramifies out until it becomes bigger than the Gospel in the minds of those responsible for it. This is the point at which the voice of Jesus reminds us to put first things first.

The Gospel is all action—redemptive action aimed at bringing the good news of salvation to all men everywhere. But any specific church activity must be criticized by the standards of its relevance to the Gospel; otherwise it is in danger of becoming mere activism.

It is not enough for the bazaar, the card-party, or the rummage sale to be held in a good cause. Martha's big supper for Jesus was held for the best of all possible causes—in theory. And today, the fact that the end product of a church activity will be more money for the church does not exempt it from the necessity of being *in itself* a vehicle of love, joy, peace, and mutual forbearance. When people push each other around in the name of the Gospel, it is a little worse than pushing each other around for some mundane goal.

Christian action is the kind of activity that brings the good news of Christ to our fellow men right here, right now. The real work of the Church is to know Christ and to make Him known by those paradigmatic actions which show forth His love and His promise of a more abundant life.

"Church work" is one thing and the work of the Church is something else. The parish is usually well organized to recruit, train, and inspire its members for church work. But how can it recruit, train, and inspire them for the real work of the Church? How can the parish relegate activity to its proper place and give first place to action?

Stir up, we beseech thee, O Lord, the wills of thy faithful people; that they, plenteously bringing forth the fruit of good works, may by thee be plenteously rewarded; through Jesus Christ our Lord. Amen.

Book of Common Prayer, page 225

There can be no doubt that the Holy Communion—the parish Eucharist—is at the heart of the matter. The ministry of the laity takes on a new dimension when the layman is thought of as "Liturgical man" or "Eucharistic man." To think of the relationship of the layman to the Church in terms of his being a name on the membership roll is to begin at the wrong end. It invites the effort to "involve" him in ushering, committee work, and other activities, until like Gulliver in Lilliput he is firmly tied down to the church by hundreds of tiny strings.

Just by being an "offerer," one who adds his "Amen" to the Eucharist, the layman is all the Christian there is or can be. Nothing can be added to the man who has received the body and blood of his Lord in Holy Communion. "Now ye are the body of Christ," says St. Paul, "and severally members thereof." Once we understand what we are, we begin to have some concept of what we ought to be doing.

The prayer quoted from *The Didache* at the end of the preceding chapter suggests why the very ancient term "Eucharist" is coming back into popularity as a name for the Holy Communion among those who are studying the significance of the service in the life of the Church. It is a word often used in the New Testament, meaning "thanksgiving." Our Lord "eucharistized" on that night before the crucifixion when He "gave thanks" and said to His disciples, "This is my body . . . this is my blood." When the Church is gathered together in response to His command, it gathers to give thanks to God for the New Covenant. And, at first it did so in forms very similar to those used by the Jewish Church to thank God for the Old Covenant and for all His blessings, including the blessing of food.

"Eucharistic man" is a new kind of human being, a participant in a new creation. The keynote of his life is thanksgiving to God for the things He has done for mankind, and in particular for the fact that in Holy Baptism we have been made a part of these things.

Nowadays, at least in this part of the world, most people are baptized in infancy and grow up surrounded by Christians. While there are many and sufficient reasons for the baptizing of infants, we need to understand baptism in its original context of an all-out decision based upon personal, conscious repentance and faith, and very probably involving conflict with family and friends and the general body of society. In Holy Baptism, we have died to one kind of life and have been reborn in another. The Holy Eucharist is the focal point on earth of the life of that new world into which we have been reborn. It is big with the overwhelming joy of redemption and vibrant with the promise of eternity.

Eucharistic man greets the past with faith, the future with hope, and the present with charity. He is not happy because he is good, but good because he is happy. This is a down-to-earth way of saying that charity is, as the theologians put it, an "infused virtue." It is not the result of something we have done, but the result of something God has done to us.

Eucharistic man can be expected to spend a certain amount of time pottering around the church, engaging in "church work." But this is, after all, a side issue for those of us who are not church professionals—a spare-time activity. Eucharistic man has to make his living, raise his family, play his part in politics and recreation. It is in these relationships that the difference between Eucharistic man and floundering man ought to be evident. It is here that the layman has a ministry, a "liturgy," a public duty, that is peculiarly his own.

The first and most fundamental thing the parish has done for him was to bring him the Gospel, to baptize him, to make him a participant in its Eucharistic worship. It has taken the load of sin and frustration and personal inadequacy off his back. Instead of tying him down with hundreds of tiny strings, it has set him free. "They that wait upon the Lord shall renew their strength; they shall mount up with wings as eagles."

And to do this, the parish has only to be itself. No program is required, except the agelong program of "the apostles' doctrine and fellowship, the breaking of the bread, and the prayers." The problem, perhaps, is to make this central program take precedence over the institutional concerns that so easily come to the fore in an activist age.

Almighty and everlasting God, give unto us the increase of faith, hope, and charity; and, that we may obtain that which thou dost promise, make us to love that which thou dost command; through Jesus Christ our Lord. Amen.

Book of Common Prayer, page 209

❋ ❋ ❋ ❋ ❋

The first job of the parish is to be itself—to be the Church. In an age of organization and activities, however, the parish is compelled to organize and carry on activities, just as it must preach the Gospel in English, if English is the language "understanded of the people." The Prayer Book Offices of Instruction put the matter in terms appropriate to our times: "My bounden duty [as a member of the Church] is to follow Christ, to worship God every Sunday in his Church; and to work and pray and give for the spread of his kingdom."

Speaking to new Christians in a different kind of civilization, I St. Peter 4 describes a Christian's duty with a different emphasis: "The end of all things is at hand; therefore keep sane and sober for your prayers. Above all hold unfailing your love for one another, since love covers a multitude of sins. Practice hospitality ungrudgingly to one another. As each has received a gift, employ it for one another, as good stewards of God's varied grace: whoever speaks, as one who utters oracles of God; whoever renders service, as one who renders it by the strength which God supplies; in order that in everything God may be glorified through Jesus Christ."

The innocent activism implied by "work and pray and give for the spread of his kingdom" would make a little better contact with the Gospel if it were "work and pray and give that in everything God may be glorified through Jesus Christ." Say God's words, work by the strength God supplies, give out of the bounty God has given you. "Let your light so shine before men . . ."

Christian action is action that reveals Christ, that by its quality as much as by its goals bears witness to the fact that we have been plucked out of a pathetic and befuddled world and planted in the community of the redeemed.

The primary lay organization of the parish church is the vestry. According to canon law, it is responsible for the fiscal side of parish life—money and property. The central lay activity of the ordinary parish church is the Every Member Canvass, the annual money-raising drive. In law, the parish is a corporation, an economic unit. In everything the vestry does as the board of directors of that corporation, money is glorified. Whether or not the vestrymen are stewards of God's varied grace, they certainly are stewards of the congregation's money.

In many Protestant denominations, the relationship between the pastor and the laity is entirely different. Predominantly lay boards sometimes have broad constitutional authority over the spiritual as well as the temporal aspects of the congregation's affairs. There the problem of the laity is not one of broadening the scope of their ministry, but of bringing it into focus upon Eucharistic worship and living. The problem of the minister under such circumstances is not one of sharing his governmental authority but of asserting his spiritual leadership.

In every Church, the time has come when the abstractions of ecumenical discussion about the ministry must be made concrete, not just in the peripheral activities of special-interest groups but in the day-to-day life of the ordinary congregation. The specifics of this process will inevitably differ in different communions. Moving toward a common norm, each must move in a different direction because it has a different starting-point.

For the Episcopal Church, the rediscovery of the laity has led many parishes to entrust to the vestry responsibilities far beyond the narrow concept of its duties as spelled out in canon law. Whether the vestry grows in this manner or not is entirely up to the parish priest. He can make them his council of advisers on a broad range of matters; or, if he chooses, he can hold them strictly to their canonical job. He must decide for himself whether he wants his lay leadership to be concerned with Christian activity or with real Christian action.

In theory, each member of the vestry is a Eucharistic man, glorifying God through Jesus Christ in his family life, his daily work, and in everything else, including his vestry service. In fact, if his role on the vestry is narrowly defined in terms of the temporalities of church life, the ministry of the laity is choked off right at the point where it should be flourishing most vigorously.

This is not a question of eternal Church principles, but of the application of those principles in today's world. It is a world not only of specialization but of ferocious competition among specialists. When a man's duties are defined, his goal is also defined. He is not supposed to take a "broad view" of the industry in which he works, but specifically to work for his own company's dominance in that industry. If he is a volunteer worker for one charity, he is commonly willing to see it prosper at the expense of another charity. Even within a single business, the man who works for one division or department is likely to fight the other divisions and departments with all his might for the greater glory of the department in which he serves.

And if he is a vestryman charged specifically with making decisions for the parish's temporal welfare, he will be quite willing to see spiritual concerns measured by their temporal effect, he will begrudge extra-parochial demands, and in all ways he will be a faithful watchdog of the parish's income and outgo in terms that would be as appropriate for an insurance company as for a unit of the kingdom of God.

In a world of specialization, accordingly, the vestry must regard itself first and foremost as a body concerned with the spiritual goals of the parish, and only secondarily as a body concerned with the temporalities of the parish. Not only must the individual vestryman be Eucharistic man, but the vestry must be a Eucharistic vestry. There is an implication here about regular church attendance by vestrymen which hardly needs further emphasis. The job of the vestryman individually, and of the vestry as a whole, is to conduct the parish's business in such a way that the Good News of redemption shines out to the world. This is a body of men charged with the overwhelming joy of redemption, invigorated by the vivid hope of eternal life. Above all, they will hold unfailing their love for one another. When a man is happy, he has no room for grudges.

The saying, "Love covers a multitude of sins" means, in the first instance, that "love is blind"—it does not hold other people's faults against them. But Christ teaches us that forgiving others and being forgiven ourselves are all of one piece. Those who love not only forgive, but are forgiven.

A vestry which is not just a board of trustees but the central planning body for the ministry of the laity—such a vestry must necessarily concern itself with the proclamation of the Gospel in the Sunday school, in the choir, among acolytes and ushers, and throughout the internal life of the parish as well as in its encounters with the world. This involves the vestry in some matters in which the parish priest is (subject to higher ecclesiastical authority) the sole arbiter. But in parishes where the priest has dared to share his responsibilities with his laymen, the results have generally been well worth the risks. A vestry concerned with the realities of religion usually measures up to its responsibilities. After all, the vestry, too, belongs to the kingdom of God.

Direct us, O Lord, in all our doings, with thy most gracious favour, and further us with thy continual help; that in all our works begun, continued, and ended in thee, we may glorify thy holy Name, and finally, by thy mercy, obtain everlasting life; through Jesus Christ our Lord. Amen.

Book of Common Prayer, page 49

The discovery that the Gospel is applicable to the business of the parish, that it is a recipe for action in this world, is the key to a broader ministry of the laity which belongs to every churchman. Here again is an opportunity for activity pointed toward action. "Daily work conferences" have been held—though usually on a diocesan or interdenominational basis—in many places. Such conferences are devoted to discussion of the relevance of Christianity to the specific jobs or professions of the people attending them. The main part of the meeting is a series of sessions according to vocational grouping—doctors with doctors, laborers with laborers, executives with executives, bankers with bankers, housewives with housewives, stenographers with stenographers, salesmen with salesmen.

In such groupings, the participants are able to view the actual conditions of their daily work in the light of the Gospel. How is a Christian banker different from a non-Christian banker? A farmer—or a clergyman—might think that bankers ought not to foreclose mortgages upon worthy people. A banker knows that mortgages sometimes have to be foreclosed, even against saints and churches. The real religious issues which confront a man who tries to be a Christian banker may be something else: the low pay scale of tellers; a pontifical, dehumanized attitude toward customers; a conflict of interest between the banker's role in the bank and his role as a corporate director.

"As in the days of Noah," they ate, they drank, they married, they were given in marriage, until the day when Noah entered the ark. The Christian (like Noah) goes on eating and drinking, marrying and giving in marriage, alongside his unheeding contemporaries. But he does so as one who knows a secret about the universe. A Christian approach to banking, for example, does not necessarily involve moving in and upsetting all the principles and practices upon which banking is based. St. John the Baptist did not tell Jews serving in the Roman army to give up soldiering. He told them (in the words of J. B. Phillips' translation of *St. Luke* 3:14): "Don't bully people, don't bring false charges, and be content with your pay."

A whole profession can and sometimes does come under the condemnation of the Gospel—as did, for example, the slave trade in the nineteenth century. Christian action can sometimes be brought to bear upon conditions within an industry—upon false advertising or sweatshop working conditions or adulteration of foods. But normally, the problem of the Christian in his daily work is to accept it pretty much as it is and within its customary framework to live as Eucharistic man.

It is within this framework that every layman has the liturgy—the "public duty"—that is peculiarly his own. This is what he offers among his brethren in the liturgy of the Church when he gives thanks before the altar.

The parish as a whole needs to be aware of what its members are doing in their economic life and to be organized to assist them in meeting their Christian problems and opportunities in this area.

But this is not an additional project for the parish to undertake—one more special interest group, having monthly get-togethers like the other guilds and societies and study classes.

The Gospel either is or is not relevant to every man's

daily work. The parish either is or is not the center from which every member goes out to bear witness to redemption in every aspect of his daily living. The Church militant is not unlike an army of a nation in this world in that it is daily involved in housekeeping tasks, in parades, inspections, and a thousand side issues. But the armies of this world are wiser than the parish in that they realize that all the side-issues are wasted unless the main issue is the ability to wage war successfully.

Almighty God, our heavenly Father, who declarest thy glory and showest forth thy handiwork in the heavens and in the earth; Deliver us, we beseech thee, in our several callings, from the service of mammon, that we may do the work which thou givest us to do, in truth, in beauty, and in righteousness, with singleness of heart as thy servants, and to the benefit of our fellow men; for the sake of him who came among us as one that serveth, thy Son Jesus Christ our Lord. Amen.

Book of Common Prayer, page 44

❋ ❋ ❋ ❋ ❋

Training, equipping, and supplying the soldiers of Christ is the main business of the parish. As such, it is the main business of the vestry. The real assets of the parish balance sheet are not its cash and real estate but men and women who know how to live as Eucharistic man.

To help the parish and its members meet their economic and social responsibilities, a "lay ministry committee," or "Christian living committee," or "social relations committee" might have a place in the parish structure along with the "finance committee," the "growth committee," the "Christian education committee," and so on. But committees concerned with Christian social relations have been notoriously short-lived and ineffectual in most places where they have been tried.

Such committees have commonly been at cross purposes with the parish goals as defined by the vestry. The vestry has been interested in "growth," in building projects, in the Sunday school, in raising money and budgeting. It is as if the establishment of army policy had been turned over to the supply services.

On the other hand, those concerned with Christian social relations in the parish, and at the diocesan and national levels as well, have often shown a good deal of the "Martha mentality" in their approach. The mere fact that they have undertaken the goal of doing good to others does not automatically guarantee that they have done so as Eucharistic man, joyfully expressing the Gospel in action. The "social gospel" of salvation by good works is as spiritually arid as the parish-centered Christianity against which it is a protest. Social action as well as parish activities can descend to the level of mere activism. Only when the life of worship and the life of redemptive action in the world become one unified whole can men see the face of Jesus Christ in the lives of His followers.

If the ministry of the laity is ever to become a central concern of the parish, the vestry itself must be the body directly and deeply involved in Christian social relations. Any committee set up to pursue this work must do so on the basis of making studies and plans for vestry implementation.

There are obvious drawbacks to this idea. In the first place, vestrymen have traditionally been one kind of person; and people interested in Christian social relations have traditionally been another kind of person. Men with a great stake in the present order of things, noted for their skill in handling money and making practical decisions according to worldly standards, have been the type considered suitable for the vestry. And social relations has been the field of those who were at war with the present order of things, the visionaries, the idealists, the revolutionaries.

Such a classification of Christians leads not only to bad vestries but to bad social relations committees. In Christ "there is neither Jew, nor Greek, there is neither bond nor free, there is neither male nor female: for ye are all one in Christ Jesus."

Once upon a time, in a hierarchical society in which every man respected and made room for his neighbor's specialty, a financial type of vestry may have been an adequate one; and it seems that such vestries did make room for the demands of idealists and revolutionaries, for there are hundreds of church institutions brought into being by the latter out of the pocketbooks of the former.

In a fluid, disintegrated society, however—and a generally more demanding, more promising, and more frightening society it is—leadership must involve the face-to-face meeting of these contrasting types of people and the hammering out of mutually acceptable policies at the conference table. The vestry must contain prophets and the social relations committee must contain financiers.

Against the disunity of the world, the Church offers the unity of the Gospel: "Ye are all one in Christ Jesus." The vestry must be representative of the varied types of people who are thus supernaturally united. It is easy for the vestry, like Martha, to become "distracted with much serving"—to think that in making much of its Lord and His Church it is offering a service pleasing to Him. His demand is much simpler, and much more difficult: that only one dish be served, but that it be served everywhere and under all possible conditions.

Grant, we beseech thee, merciful God, that thy Church, being gathered together in unity by thy Holy Spirit, may manifest thy power among all peoples, to the glory of thy Name; through Jesus Christ our Lord, who liveth and reigneth with thee and the same Spirit, one God, world without end. Amen.

Book of Common Prayer, page 185

* * 7 * *

Redefining Christian Social Relations

IN THE preceding chapter, a parish concern with "lay ministry," or with "Christian living," or with "Christian social relations" was regarded essentially as a concern with one thing. And although these three terms are not perfectly synonymous, the fact that they do very largely cover the same ground is one of the significant discoveries of Christian thought in our times.

"Christian living" is the most inclusive of the three. Christian living is everybody's business. As Christians, we have a new relationship with God and with our fellow men. This new relationship enters into every area of our lives, and the working out of its implications in terms of both general principles and specific situations is the subject-matter of Christian living.

"The ministry of the laity," or "lay ministry," refers specifically to the things a Christian is supposed to *do* as a result of his new relationship to God and man. He

has a ministry, or service, to perform for both. Christian living includes the internal life of the individual Christian as well as his outward responsibilities, whereas the ministry of the laity deals primarily with the latter.

But to the Christian, living and ministering are inseparable. "You know," said Jesus, "that the rulers of the Gentiles lord it over them, and their great men exercise authority among them. It shall not be so among you; but whoever would be great among you must be your servant, and whoever would be first among you must be your slave." We are lifted up to God only by the hands of our fellow men, and approach Him only as we help them to climb with us. The ministry of the laity, too, is everybody's business. *Personal religion is genuine Christianity only when the word "person" is plural.*

"Christian social relations" has been in the past almost a technical term for certain special areas of Christian concern. Things done by the more fortunate for the less fortunate—Christmas baskets for the poor, orphanages, old-age homes, hospitals, settlement houses, counselling services, refugee relief, services to alcoholics —such things as these are classified as Christian social relations under the general heading of health and welfare services. Another area of Christian social relations is the marshalling of Church opinion to deal with broad political and social issues, under the heading of social education and action, or Christian citizenship.

In recent years, a third area of Christian concern has been included in Christian social relations under the heading of urban-industrial church work. This area deals with the preaching of the Gospel under the peculiar conditions that confront many American cities—poverty, loss of membership to the suburbs, residential blight, racial and cultural conflict, etc. This again seems to be a part of Christian social relations because it is a ministry paid for by the more fortunate and intended to benefit the less fortunate.

In the Episcopal Church, there is a national Department of Christian Social Relations with its appropriate divisions of Health and Welfare, Christian Citizenship, and Urban-Industrial Church Work. Many dioceses have similar departments and divisions. Sometimes a parish attempts a similar department or committee, but usually the committee runs out of vitality after a year or two and dies.

A part of the reason is the tendency of the parish to be a success-institution. But another part of the reason is the fact that Christian social relations as conceived in the past has not been a valid part of the day-in, day-out parish program.

It doesn't matter in the least whether parishes have Christian social relations committees. But it does matter greatly whether parishes present a valid and full-bodied Gospel that includes the kind of concern for man's physical, mental, social, and economic problems that gives rise to national and diocesan programs.

In a sense, national and diocesan social service programs are not really Gospel. They represent Christian love at the end of a ten-foot pole, a refusal of the Christian community to become intimately involved with human wretchedness and social conflict. To the parish the financial support of these remote diocesan and national programs is likely to represent a form of insurance against social upheaval rather than the outstretched arms of brother to brother.

Those who are actively engaged in the work of Christian social relations are acutely aware of this serious criticism of the basic presuppositions of their work. Much of what has been thought and written about the ministry of the laity has been spurred by an effort to redefine Christian social relations and reorient its goals so that it may, whether nationally or locally, be rooted in the day-to-day life of the Christian community and be genuine Gospel.

The Gospel is social. It deals with relations among men and between men and God. The parish is a social institution, existing in a social setting, making known the good news of Christ through its own actions, or failing to do so. These are some of the ingredients of a redefinition of Christian social relations which will have to be worked out in practice as parishes come to grips with the full meaning of Christian living and the ministry of the laity.

O Lord, our heavenly Father, whose blessed Son came not to be ministered unto, but to minister; We beseech thee to bless all who, following in his steps, give themselves to the service of their fellow men. Endue them with wisdom, patience, and courage to strengthen the weak and raise up those who fall; that, being inspired by thy love, they may worthily minister in thy Name to the suffering, the friendless, and the needy; for the sake of him who laid down his life for us, the same thy Son, our Saviour Jesus Christ. Amen.

Book of Common Prayer, page 43

This seems to be chiefly a prayer for the "professionals" of Christian social service. God grant that it may become a prayer for every layman in his Christian vocation.

* * * * *

Another aspect of the ministry of the laity is "evangelism." This, like "Christian social relations," has become almost a technical term. Its root meaning is "good-news-ism"—proclaiming the Gospel. Its specific meaning is the winning of new members for the parish church.

Unlike social relations, evangelism is not the special responsibility of any department or division of Episcopal Church headquarters. In a sense, it does not need to be. Today's parishes are quite adept at winning new members. If they were not, they would soon fade out of existence, for 10% of the members of the typical American parish move away every year.

Understood in its basic and deepest sense, evangelism is the main business of the Church and of the laity. But, as this business is carried on today it sometimes becomes almost a caricature of the Gospel—a recognizable, but distorted, and perhaps even a ludicrous, picture.

Even an unregenerate vestry understands the value of an evangelism committee—a "growth" committee. Its purpose is to make the parish a bigger and better institution, to provide more volunteers for parish projects, more income, more leadership. If social relations belongs to the spending side of church life, evangelism belongs to the getting side.

Under the growth concept, it is unquestionably evangelism to win a new member from some other Christian communion. It may even be evangelism to win a member from another parish of one's own Church.

Since God is no respecter of persons, the enthusiast for church growth argues, He ought to be just as happy over the conversion of a lawyer or business executive as over the conversion of a day-laborer or relief client. Since the former can do more for the parish than the latter, the growth committee instinctively concentrates on the "right kind of people," so that there will be rejoicing not only in heaven but on earth over the sinner that repenteth.

Evangelism is the main business of the Church. That is generally agreed. What, then, is the place of Christian social service in the view of the individual or parish that regards evangelism as church growth? Social service is all right if it brings in new members, either in the form of grateful clients or in the form of people of good will who think that the Church, like the Elks Club or the Shriners, ought to be doing something useful. Otherwise, to engage in social service is to dissipate church energies that ought to be expended instead upon evangelism.

Even among dedicated Christians who have risen far above the narrow concept of the parish as a place for "our kind of people," this question is a troubling one. Evangelism consists of taking people who are not Christians and making them Christians. If it takes $10,000-worth of social service to make one convert, and only $100-worth of evangelism, which expenditure is the better Christian stewardship?

This is the crucial issue. It is the thing that sharply

marks off the activist call to "work and pray and give for the spread of his kingdom" from St. Peter's "as each has received a gift, employ it for one another, as good stewards of God's varied grace." It sets the notion that we can do something for God in contrast with the truth that God has done something for us which gives us a new relationship with our fellow man. Certainly give him theology, give him baptism, give him the right hand of fellowship; but by all means, if you meet him dazed and beaten on the road, bind up his wounds! The one thing is just as much "gospel" as the other. It is the tragedy of our times that the parish understands the relation of the one to the altar of God and fails to understand the relationship of the other.

The love of souls becomes a greed for souls, when the bodies in which souls dwell are neglected. Like the angels who fell from heaven, the parish has stopped at the contemplation of its own spiritual good and does not look up to see the needs of humanity reflected in the eyes of Christ.

Christ tells us what we can do for God. We can feed Him when He is hungry. We can give Him a drink when He is thirsty, take Him in when He is friendless, clothe Him when He is naked, visit Him when He is sick, care for Him when He is in prison. This is our part in spreading the kingdom of God—those paradigmatic actions whereby reason, light, and compassion break for a moment through the clouds of sin. He Himself will see to the harvest of souls. He Himself will bring in the kingdom while His Church stands around in confusion and fear and trembling.

Bringing people into the Church is only one part of

evangelism. The whole of evangelism involves the whole of the Gospel—so living and healing and saving and ministering that *in everything* God may be glorified through Jesus Christ.

Almighty and everlasting God, who art always more ready to hear than we to pray, and art wont to give more than either we desire or deserve; Pour down upon us the abundance of thy mercy; forgiving us those things whereof our conscience is afraid, and giving us those good things we are not worthy to ask, but through the merits and mediation of Jesus Christ, thy Son, our Lord. Amen.

Book of Common Prayer, page 206

Another aspect of the work of the Church against which Christian social relations must redefine itself is missions. Missions shares with social relations a connotation of being for "the other people" as opposed to evangelism, which is understood to be for "people like ourselves." It shares with evangelism, however, the connotation of being directly concerned with the Gospel instead of being, as social relations is supposed to be, a frill or an extra.

Actually, as informed churchpeople well know, the Church has one world-embracing mission, summed up in the words that conclude the Gospel according to St. Matthew: "Go ye therefore, and teach all nations, baptizing them in the name of the Father and of the Son, and of the Holy Ghost: teaching them to observe all things whatsoever I have commanded you: and, lo, I am with you alway, even unto the end of the world."

"Missions" are specific assignments for the carrying out of this single mission.

In the mission fields, it seems that the unity of the Church's evangelistic task is quickly understood and exhibited. A hospital, a school, a clinic, an orphanage in an underprivileged land is an obvious and inevitable expression of the Gospel. The answer to the question, "What is the God of the Christians like?" must necessarily be, "He is One who cares for you and for all that affects you." Indeed, there is so strong a cultural and social aspect to the work of the overseas missionary that he has to be on his guard lest he turn out to be a missionary for American culture instead of for Christ. The secular know-how of an advanced civilization tends to be exported via missionary channels. And sometimes what goes along with the know-how is irrelevant. Episcopalian missionaries have not been notably insistent on European clothing in non-European lands. But somehow, in the past, the houses of worship erected for their congregations have often looked as if they had been transported bodily from the American or English countryside.

In missionary fields, leaving people to work out their own social and cultural techniques as much as possible may be as important an insight of social relations as the urge to help them. The insistence that the Gospel is for the whole of man serves as a reminder that it is for the whole of all kinds of men, for different degrees of civilization, for varied patterns of social organization and different stages of economic development.

The parish itself is a "mission field," in the sense that the clergy and laity of each parish are responsible for the carrying forward of the Church's mission in that particular city or suburb or neighborhood. Its concern with the mission of the Church in other areas is a simple act of recognition that the Gospel is for everybody everywhere and that each of us is involved in an enterprise that is relevant to all of us.

Accordingly, the basic role of social relations in the parish and in the mission field is the same. It reveals what kind of God we worship, it reflects His concern for the whole of life, it gives expression to the impulses grafted into Eucharistic man as the result of his being grafted into the vine that is Christ.

In the field of propaganda, the material and the evangelistic aspects of the Church's mission claim credit from each other. "Why do you try to convert people from their happy pagan ways?" is countered with the assertion that the Gospel brings them a more abundant life in this world. Their pagan ways are not quite so happy as the romantic movies might suggest. "Why do you spend so much missionary time and money on material aid to your people?" is answered by the statement that only thus can they be spiritually converted to Christ. "You can't preach to people with empty stomachs," is the old saying, and it is half true. You can't preach persuasively to people with empty stomachs unless your stomach is also empty.

But if the missionary's stomach is empty too, he is very likely to find himself turning up in the hunger-march along with his people. Either way, he is preaching some Gospel, some good news, about bread.

As the work of bringing the Gospel to bodies, minds, and souls is all one in the mission field, so also it is in the parish. The mission of the parish, too, is to share the condition of those whom it would serve—and, if their condition is one which nobody in his right mind would share, to fight for its betterment.

Christian social relations cannot be defined "against" missions. It is *integral* to the Church's mission—as a present fact, in the fields overseas; and, in the parish, as something to be learned, and from the mission fields made a fact of parish life.

O God, the Creator and Preserver of all mankind, we humbly beseech thee for all sorts and conditions of men; that thou wouldest be pleased to make thy ways known unto them, thy saving health unto all nations. More especially we pray for thy holy Church universal; that it may be so guided and governed by thy good Spirit, that all who profess and call themselves Christians may be led into the way of truth, and hold the faith in unity of spirit, in the bond of peace, and in righteousness of life. Finally, we commend to thy fatherly goodness all those who are in any ways afflicted, or distressed, in mind, body, or estate; that it may please thee to comfort and relieve them, according to their several necessities; giving them patience under their sufferings, and a happy issue out of all their afflictions. And this we beg for Jesus Christ's sake. Amen.

Book of Common Prayer, page 18

* * * * *

One of the great social facts of modern America is the breakdown of the old system of social classes under the sustained assault of democratic idealism. The belief in human freedom, equality, and brotherhood has been vigorously taught and put into practice to a degree undreamed of in any other nation in history.

The result is that today, while social stratifications continue to exist, the individual passes quickly and easily from one vaguely defined class to another. Many things help in the determination of social status—birth, breeding, place of residence, type of work, financial power, political opinions, friendships, etc.—but no one thing guarantees the individual a secure place in the social scale. He can rise, or fall, overnight.

There are many good things about this powerful drive for social democracy. In some measure, it is a genuine expression for our times of the dynamics of the Gospel. But men are still sinners, still earth-bound creatures, and their relations with each other do not express the perfect charity of the kingdom of God in the present class structure any more than they did in older civilizations with strong and static social classes.

People still need to know where they stand in relation to their fellow men. They need to know who are their equals, who are their betters, and who are their inferiors. To attain this status, the great American expedient is the neighborhood, with its purified refinement, the suburb. If we cannot be equals with everybody, at least we can be equals with our neighbors, living in homes of similar price and architectural taste, bringing up our children among children who will ultimately be suitable marriage partners for them, shopping at the same stores, reading the same kind of books, enjoying the same kind of recreation and entertainment, and—attending the same kind of church.

Once upon a time, the Church of Christ was planted

in a neighborhood as the meeting place of all classes of men who lived in that neighborhood. Aristocrat and commoner, mistress and maid, merchant and apprentice, black man and white man lived in close proximity, separated by invisible but universally known and accepted barriers of class. Though their inequality on the natural level was taken for granted, they were all equals at the altar of God.

Now, the churches fulfill an unsought role in social relations by serving as one of the many instruments of social stratification. The more they try to express their members' supernatural equality in Christ in the program of Sunday school, guild, and other church activities, the more the congregations respond by instinctively seeking out a church consisting as much as possible of their social equals. While there is a modicum of truth in attaching social status to whole denominations, the variations from one congregation to another in any one of the old, well-established churches are much more significant.

There is nothing essentially wicked about the existence of a community resource for sorting people out into congenial types. But to have the Church of Jesus Christ fall into the trap of serving as this kind of community resource comes close to being a denial of the Gospel.

The Church is the place where human beings are equal, not because of their equal powers, abilities, tastes, and standards, but because of their equal lowliness and insignificance before God. It is the place where men accept each other, not because of their acceptability, but because Christ accepts them. Its camaraderie is not that of a social club but that of an army or a baseball crowd —the sharing of a great common task, the enjoyment of a great common enthusiasm. The very word enthusiasm means "in-god-ness."

Thus, the parish that is unconscious of the significance of Christian social relations tends to become the servant of another kind of social relations that shrewdly assaults its validity and integrity as a unit of the body of Christ. By failing to cope with the social meaning of the Gospel, it begins to lose its grip on the personal meaning of the Gospel.

The Church is not interested in the distinction between "our kind of people" and "the other kind of people." It is interested only in Christ's kind of people. "If any man is in Christ, he is a new creature." The only social status that is relevant to the Church's interests is a man's status as a member of Christ, a child of God, and an inheritor of the kingdom of heaven.

O God, who hast made of one blood all nations of men for to dwell on the face of the whole earth, and didst send thy blessed Son to preach peace to them that are far off and to them that are nigh; Grant that all men everywhere may seek after thee and find thee. Bring the nations into thy fold, pour out thy Spirit upon all flesh, and hasten thy kingdom; through the same thy Son Jesus Christ our Lord. Amen.

Book of Common Prayer, page 38

* * * * *

A meaningful definition of Christian social relations at the parish level would be: the training, equipping, and supplying of the people of God to bear witness to the Gospel in every aspect of their life among their fellow men. There is no difference in subject matter here from the work of evangelism when evangelism is understood in its widest and deepest meaning; nor is there any basic difference in subject matter from the mission of the Church, which is to bring the Gospel to all men and all nations and groupings of men.

The special concern of Christian social relations, however, is the impact of the Gospel upon people's relationships with each other—their social relations. These extend from the daily concerns of family life and work and play to the problems of the local community and state and all the way up to the great issues of national and international affairs.

The Gospel is for all men, for all nations, for the world of nature and the worlds beyond worlds. The Gospel does not exist for the Church. It is the other way around: The Church exists to proclaim the Gospel. The Church is interested in the price of bread, in the purity of the water supply, the loneliness of the aged, the prosperity of the garment industry, the development of antibiotics, and the probation and parole system, because the Gospel is about these things.

Once upon a time, in the days of the social Gospel, it was thought that the high goal of Christian social relations was to "Christianize the social order." This grandiose conception both overrates the abilities of men and misconceives the Christian interpretation of history. The good news we have to tell is (1) that God has revealed His redemptive purpose and power in Jesus Christ; and (2) He is preparing a new order of things in which He Himself will complete that redemptive purpose.

This good news is proclaimed here and now in the social order not by the elaboration of some great scheme to bring sin to an end by human efforts, but by those paradigmatic actions, those fragments of the Gospel that convey the taste of the whole.

The task of the Christian is not to christianize the social order, but to evangelize the social order. He is not reconstructing the world, but expressing Christ's charity within it.

An editorial in *Life* magazine created a memorable phrase a few years ago when it said that the President of the United States "cannot be a kind of Calif Haroun el Raschid, dispensing random rescues and arbitrary blessings." This is undoubtedly very sound advice to a government, but random rescues and arbitrary blessings are the very warp and woof of Christian social relations. They are the clues scattered about on the trail of Christ, the signs that He has touched the lives of twentieth-century men and women, the evidence of the comprehensive sweep of His redemptive purpose, the pledges of His love.

Thus, the place where it is vitally important for social relations—relations between people—to bear the marks of the Gospel is in the parish and in the man-to-man relationships of Christians with each other and with their fellow men. Wider social concerns, if they are to be truly paradigmatic, must spring out of the down-to-earth concerns of the people of God about making some piece of the good news meaningful in the lives of some real people.

Christian social relations is the training, equipping, and supplying of the people of God to bear witness to the Gospel in every aspect of their life among their fellow men.

O God, Almighty and merciful, who healest those that are broken in heart, and turnest the sadness of the sorrowful to joy; Let thy fatherly goodness be upon all that thou hast made. Remember in pity such as are this day destitute, homeless, or forgotten of their fellow-men. Bless the congregation of thy poor. Uplift those who are cast down. Mightily befriend innocent sufferers, and sanctify to them the endurance of their wrongs. Cheer with hope all discouraged and unhappy people, and by thy heavenly grace preserve from falling those whose penury tempteth them to sin; though they be troubled on every side, suffer them not to be distressed; though they be perplexed, save them from despair. Grant this, O Lord, for the love of him, who for our sakes became poor, thy Son, our Saviour Jesus Christ. Amen.

Book of Common Prayer, page 599

* * 8 * *

Encountering the Cross

ONE OF THE most beautiful paradigmatic anecdotes about Jesus in the New Testament is the story of the woman taken in adultery. There was no doubt about her guilt, nor about the legal penalty of stoning that was due her. It seemed to the scribes and Pharisees a good opportunity to place what Jesus stood for against the commandments of the Mosaic law and the instincts of all right-thinking people.

So they brought her to Him and asked Him what He thought should be done with her. After a brief silence, He replied: "Let him who is without sin among you be the first to throw a stone at her."

"But when they heard it, they went away, one by one, beginning with the eldest, and Jesus was left alone with the woman standing before him. Jesus looked up and said to her: 'Woman, where are they? Has no one condemned you?' She said, 'No one, Lord.' And Jesus said, 'Neither do I condemn you; go, and do not sin again.'" (*St. John* 8:1-11, RSV)

Professor A. T. Mollegen once referred to this story as an example of the eschatological element in the Gospel. It cannot be used, he said, to establish the general principle that society must give up protecting itself against the lawbreaker. Rather, the general principle involved is that Jesus and the Gospel stand in judgment over the justice of this world, that the pillars of society and the notorious sinners are alike in their need for forgiveness and redemption.

One of his students sharply disagreed with the implication that Christians could not follow the example of Jesus in dealing with the lawbreaker. But, a year or two later, after he was graduated and serving as a chaplain on a college campus, he had an opportunity to try.

The young chaplain was walking down a street of the college town one day when he saw a group of students milling around outside a cheap hotel and looking up at one of the windows. He looked up and saw a young woman of doubtful occupation and undoubted intoxication starting to take her clothes off while the students hooted and shouted encouragement. The chaplain sprinted up the hotel stairs and joined the young woman in the window, arguing earnestly that she should stop making a spectacle of herself. The addition of a clergyman to the scene delighted the spectators below, and the young woman continued with her performance.

In spite of his belief in the superiority of forgiveness to mere law enforcement, the chaplain was never so glad to see a policeman in his life as he was when one turned up to see what all the noise was about and arrested the woman and packed her off to jail.

But the chaplain was not done. The next day he went

to the jail and offered to pay the woman's fine for her. She refused his offer with contempt and profanity.

Not long afterward he saw Dr. Mollegen again and told him the story. "Now," he said, "I know what you mean by the difficulties of trying to imitate the eschatological actions of Jesus."

The gospel of service to men's social needs does not necessarily get any better hearing from those it would seek to help than the verbal proclamation of the Church's faith. When Eucharistic man carries the love of God into action in home or shop or public street, he may be doing no visible good either to the Church or to the person he is trying to help. What is good news to one person may be bad news to another; the saying, "It is more blessed to give than to receive" often has a wry application in the reaction of those who are made the objects of other people's kindness.

Here again, we need to remember that it is not the job of the Christian to solve all the problems of the world and bring in the kingdom of God. It is his job to reflect, as brightly as his own sins and limitations will permit, the divine glory that has been freely poured out upon him.

In the words of St. Paul's Second Epistle to the Corinthians as vividly translated by J. B. Phillips: "All of us who are Christians have no veils on our faces, but reflect like mirrors the glory of the Lord. We are transfigured by the Spirit of the Lord in ever-increasing splendor into his own image. . . . If our Gospel is "veiled," the veil must be in the minds of those who are spiritually dying. The spirit of this world has blinded the minds of those who do not believe, and prevents the light of the glorious Gospel of Christ, the image of God, from shining on them. "For it is Christ Jesus the Lord whom we preach, not ourselves. . . . God, who first ordered light to shine in the darkness, has flooded our hearts with his light. We can now enlighten men only because we can give them knowledge of the glory of God as we see it in the face of Jesus Christ."

To know Christ is to make Him known. And, sometimes, it is to be crucified with Him.

Almighty and everlasting God, who, of thy tender love towards mankind, hast sent thy Son, our Saviour Jesus Christ, to take upon him our flesh, and to suffer death upon the cross, that all mankind should follow the example of his great humility; Mercifully grant, that we may both follow the example of his patience, and also be made partakers of his resurrection; through the same Jesus Christ our Lord. Amen.

Book of Common Prayer, page 134

✻ ✻ ✻ ✻ ✻

"Happy are those who know that they are needy," says Jesus. "I have some good news for them."

(When the King James translators rendered the Greek word meaning "happy"—*makarios*—as "blessed," they did not know that later generations would draw a distinction between happiness and blessedness.)

"Happy are the mourners, for I have comfort for them."

"Happy are the gentle people; for I will give them the world."

"Happy are those who are hungry and thirsty for righteousness; I have some good news for them."

"Happy are the merciful; for I will give them mercy."

"Happy are the pure in heart; for I will give them the vision of God."

"Happy are the peacemakers; for they shall be my brothers."

"Happy are those who suffer for the sake of righteousness; I have some good news for them."

"Happy are you when you get into deep trouble on account of me and my good news. . . ."

There are few counsels of moderation in the Gospel. Christ's followers are occasionally told not to beat their heads against a stone wall, not to spread their treasures before those who despise them. But when *The Didache*, or "Teaching of the Apostles," says, "Let thine alms sweat into thine hands until thou shalt have learned to whom to give," it is sliding downhill from the New Testament standard. It is making a reasonable compromise between the demands of the Gospel and the demands of common sense.

And so, no doubt, must we all, including the unfortunate young college chaplain. The pigeons on the courthouse steps obviously have to snatch a few more mouthfuls of corn before stretching their wings and making a tentative try toward the journey home. The Gospel beats against our bastions of prudence as the waves beat against the towering cliffs along the shore of the ocean. We know that the ocean will win—but let it be tomorrow, rather than today. Our prayer is like that of the small child: "Lord, make me a good boy—but not yet." Let us set aside happiness for later on. Right now, we prefer to stay preoccupied and confused.

Almighty God, whose most dear Son went not up to joy but first he suffered pain, and entered not into glory before he was crucified; Mercifully grant that we, walking in the way of the cross, may find it none other than the way of life and peace; through the same thy Son Jesus Christ our Lord. Amen.

Book of Common Prayer, page 138

* * * * *

It is true of the individual layman, as it is of the parish, that he has to choose between being "in the world but not of it" or "of the world but not in it." The worldly man who owes no allegiance to Christ can be both in and of the world, dealing effectively with the world in terms of the world's own values. The Christian, however, is in the world to heal it; if he tries to be merely a part of the world, merely a successful and respected citizen, his acceptance of the world's values makes him ineffectual in his task of ministering in the world according to the standard of the Beatitudes.

There is a fundamental conflict between the world and the Gospel, and the only way for a Christian to escape from the wounds and fatigue of battle is to become a prisoner of the world. Christianity offers a way through trouble, not a way out of it.

The great lie that dominates much of church life today is the belief that the layman is a part-time Christian and the clergyman is a full-time Christian. The priest who spends every waking hour in the service of the Church must face every Gospel-denying pressure that is known to the laity, every sin, every compromise, every surrender to the world's values and standards. The Church buys and sells, hires and fires; it competes, lobbies, uses influence, defends its privileges like any other institution of the world.

If living in the world is what requires a man to be a part-time Christian, then we are all part-time Christians, clergy and laity alike, and the parish is only a part-time witness to the Gospel.

The truth is that there is only one way to be a Christian—the full-time way. The more vigorously you are involved in the affairs of the world, the richer your opportunities for bearing witness to the Gospel.

The revolutionaries who serve other lords take this fact for granted. Communists do not begrudge the service of their "laity" in key positions in society. In fact, the Communist Party is eager to get them into such positions in the confidence that, whatever they may be doing, they will be serving the Communist cause. Similarly, the assumption should be that almost any position in the world is a good place for serving the Christian cause.

Most of the time, the Christian and the world get along together pretty well. It is only occasionally that an issue comes up that reveals the fundamental conflict, showing up the Christian as one whose basic loyalties lie outside the business or the club or the union or the trade association. But this is the moment that matters. "Blessed are ye when men shall revile you, and persecute you, and shall say all manner of evil against you falsely, for my sake. Rejoice, and be exceeding glad: for great is your reward in heaven: for so persecuted they the prophets which were before you."

The first eyewitness account outside the New Testament of a Christian martyrdom is the epistle of the church at Smyrna about the death of its Bishop, Polycarp. The epistle is at great pains to point out that Polycarp did not seek out martyrdom. In fact, it is rather caustic about a few who fanatically turned themselves in and then recanted under torture.

"Picking a fight" with the world is one thing. Standing firm against the world's hostility is something else. There is a kind of aggressive piety, the slogans of the Gospel ever on its lips, answering questions before they are asked, wielding the grace of God like a club, that confuses the issue of Christian witness today as the eager, would-be martyrs of Smyrna confused the issue in Polycarp's day.

Yet, when the test does come, when the issue really is drawn, then we are to rejoice and be exceeding glad; for the experience of the Cross is at the very heart of the Gospel.

O Lord God, whose blessed Son, our Saviour, gave his back to the smiters and hid not his face from shame; Grant us grace to take joyfully the sufferings of the present time, in full assurance of the glory that shall be revealed; through the same thy Son Jesus Christ our Lord. Amen.

Book of Common Prayer, page 144

* * * * *

The Cross is at the heart of the Gospel, both as a fact of history and as a part of the experience of the individual Christian.

The cross of Christian experience—the individual's

cross—would be just one more example of the tragic element in life without the Cross of Christ. We tend to interpret His Cross by our own, to deal with the crucifixion subjectively. This is a sound act of Christian devotion which may help us to value the objective, historical meaning of His Cross more highly. Yet the latter meaning is the one that counts.

Lincoln, in the Gettysburg address, touched upon the theme of self-sacrifice in words which will have a universal application in the realm of human affairs as long as brave men continue to face death for a cause. But a vital question in connection with the Gettysburg address is, "Who won?" Today, the main point of that great exposition of the meaning of sacrifice is that the sacrifice accomplished its intended purpose.

Lost causes have their own poetry and dignity—a certain ideal existence that sometimes makes the losers more glamorous than their opponents who won and had to face the humdrum responsibilities and ugly temptations of victory. Nevertheless, the first and most important question about every battle is, "Who won it?"

"The world will little note, nor long remember, what we say here," said Lincoln, "but it can never forget what they did here." So the Church holds up for remembrance what Jesus *did* on Calvary as the victory which won a new birth of freedom for all men everywhere.

The fulness of the meaning of that victory is beyond the power of theology to explain. At-one-ment—reconciliation—between mankind and God is the name that is given to it. Different generations have attempted different explanations of the atonement in accordance with the cultural patterns of their time and place. But the atonement is explained most graphically in those paradigmatic actions of seeking and saving, healing and feeding, forgiving and releasing, which marked the trial of the Son of man in His earthly sojourn.

"Random rescues and arbitrary blessings" accompanied the preaching of the kingdom. When a sower sows his seed at random some of it sprouts, some of it doesn't, some of the seedlings wither, and some grow up to harvest and bear fruit a hundredfold. But you know one thing about the sower. He is looking for a harvest. You can tell what kind of harvest by looking at the seeds he is sowing. The saving actions of Jesus among men revealed the saving purpose of the Lord of the Harvest.

But when Jesus set His face "like a flint" to go up to Jerusalem, the whole question of repentance and acceptance of the kingdom of God became a question of here and now. Everybody who had a stake in the world that was dying was faced with the necessity of choosing between that world and the world of life and immortality.

He entered the city as a king, riding in triumphal procession. Kings often chose to ride on donkeys in those days. The donkey did not symbolize the lack of royal pomp or dignity, but rather the peaceful intentions of the king. In today's terms, He arrived in an open convertible instead of in an armored car.

Peaceful or not, His arrival put the city into an uproar and His cleansing of the Temple and forthright preaching about the kingdom of God drew the issue ever more sharply. The hostility of the powerful, the indifference of the many, and the timidity of His disciples converged to bring about the predictable result. He was betrayed, captured, interrogated, condemned, and killed.

This is the inevitable story of the fate of love, peace, and righteousness in a world under the dominion of sin. Tomorrow always seems to be a better time than today for declaring our allegiance to the kingdom of God.

But the story did not end there. The King whom mankind had rejected was vindicated by God. "This Jesus hath God raised up," said St. Peter in the first proclamation of the Gospel on Pentecost. ". . . Therefore, let all the house of Israel know assuredly that God hath made that same Jesus, whom ye crucified, both Lord and Christ."

Perhaps the deepest statement of the meaning of the victory of Christ is in St. Paul's Epistle to the Philippians.

"Have this mind among yourselves, which you have in Christ Jesus, who, though he was in the form of God, did not count equality with God a thing to be grasped, but emptied himself, taking the form of a servant, being born in the likeness of men. And being found in human form he humbled himself and became obedient unto death, even death on a cross. Therefore God has highly exalted him and bestowed on him the name which is above every name, that at the name of Jesus every knee should bow, in heaven and on earth and under the earth, and every tongue confess that Jesus Christ is Lord, to the glory of God the Father.

"Therefore, my beloved . . . work out your own salvation with fear and trembling; for God is at work in you, both to will and to work for his good pleasure." (*Philippians* 2:5-13, RSV.)

And the fruit of that victory in which we share is the

atonement, the restored relationship with God, won for us by Christ.

The disaster of mankind's rejection of God's love is the measure of the vastness of His steadfast purpose to win in spite of ourselves.

Assist us mercifully with thy help, O Lord God of our salvation; that we may enter with joy upon the meditation of those mighty acts, whereby thou has given unto us life and immortality; through Jesus Christ our Lord. Amen.

Book of Common Prayer, page 147

❋ ❋ ❋ ❋ ❋

It is the Cross of Christ that brings salvation, not the personal crosses we must bear as His followers. The victory is still His even when we meet frustration or stumble and fall as we try to follow in His steps.

In an earlier chapter, the significance of the Holy Communion as a "memorial" was touched upon in terms of our becoming participants in Christ's atoning life. There is a further significance to the word "memorial" as applied to the Holy Communion, for it is a memorial before God as well as man. We pray that the Father will "little note nor long remember" our halting efforts to do His will, remembering instead what Jesus did in His life and death of perfect obedience.

"Look, Father, look on his anointed face,
And only look on us as found in him;
Look not on our misusings of thy grace,
Our prayer so languid, and our faith so dim;
For lo! between our sins and their reward,
We set the passion of thy Son our Lord."

So says the communion hymn ("And now, O Father, mindful of the love") which has been described as almost a sufficient prayer of consecration in itself. The thing we really have to offer to the Father in our worship is not our own merits but our "in-Christ-ness." "Ourselves, our souls and bodies" become "a reasonable, holy, and living sacrifice" *only* as the result of our being "made one body with Him."

So, the service of Holy Communion is a "memorial" in a sense similar to the use of the word for a petition addressed to government—a "memorandum," a "reminder" before God of the new covenant established by Christ at the Last Supper when He said, "This is the New Covenant in my blood."

Almighty Father, whose dear Son, on the night before he suffered, did institute the Sacrament of his Body and Blood; Mercifully grant that we may thankfully receive the same in remembrance of him, who in these holy mysteries giveth us a pledge of life eternal; the same thy Son Jesus Christ our Lord, who now liveth and reigneth with thee and the Holy Spirit ever, one God, world without end. Amen.

Book of Common Prayer, page 152

Viewed in the light of the Cross, the concept of "the ministry of the laity" is forced to assume more realistic proportions. It is true that when we try to bring the good news of Christ to our fellow men they do not always respond to it as we had hoped. When Jesus Himself proclaimed the Good News of the kingdom, mankind's response was "Let him be crucified." There is no particular reason for His followers to expect a different response.

But in the light of the Cross we see an even more unpalatable fact. A certain bishop has a sign on his desk that asks his visitors: "Have you got a solution or are you just part of the problem?" In the great enterprise of bringing salvation to mankind, the individual Christian is a part of the problem quite as much as he is a part of its solution.

We are those whom the King has requisitioned from the highways and hedges: the lame, the halt, and the blind whom He has rounded up to share in His supper. His kingdom is not something we spread by our working, praying, and giving; it is something into which we are gathered, gasping like fish in a net. At the feast, He supplies us with the wedding garment of forgiveness and all we have to have is the grace to put it on.

Yet, He has chosen to give us the dignity of being participants in His life and in His ministry; to make us sharers not only in His joy but in His struggles and sufferings. There are souls that will not be saved unless we save them, wounds that will not be healed unless we heal them, mouths that will not be fed unless we feed them.

And there are frustrations and sorrows reserved for each of those who, having taken on this ministry, find that it doesn't always work. The experience of the Cross in the life of the Christian is not just a matter of facing the hostility and indifference of the world. It is also a matter of facing the apparent hostility and indifference of the forces of righteousness, of the universe itself.

The Cross is not just the wounds of honest warfare; it is the dirty trick that life plays upon us, the unfair and unexpected blow from our friends. For the layman, the Cross may be the attitude of his parish priest; for the priest, it may be a decision of the bishop. We know the Cross when God Himself seems to have withdrawn from the situation and left us to suffer the consequences of trying to do His will.

It is here that we enter most deeply into the mystery of the sufferings of Christ. It is not so hard to be glad when we suffer for something we deserve; it is not too hard to summon up the heroism and self-giving to die for a cause; but to face the death of the cause itself is to face the possibility that life has no meaning at all.

The cry, "My God, my God, why hast thou forsaken me?" implies such a facing, not merely of personal defeat, but of the defeat of the cause of righteousness. Yet this is the point at which defeat is turned into victory and death is turned into resurrection. God's saving purpose requires none of the success involved in the pursuit of worldly purposes, but only faith expressed in obedience to, and through, the end.

Almighty God, we beseech thee graciously to behold this thy family, for which our Lord Jesus Christ was contented to be betrayed, and given up into the hands of wicked men, and to suffer death upon the cross; who now liveth and reigneth with thee and the Holy Ghost ever, one God, world without end. Amen.

Book of Common Prayer, page 156

❋ ❋ ❋ ❋ ❋

"May grace come and may this world pass away." This call for the lowering of the curtain upon the stage of history in the prayer previously quoted from *The Didache* (p. 84) is a paraphrase of the petition, "Thy kingdom come," in the Lord's Prayer. It is a sobering thought that in church and at home, millions of twentieth-century Christians are constantly praying for the end of the world.

A first-century Christian could not say, "Thy kingdom come," with the coolness of the twentieth-century Christian nor even with the cheerful enthusiasm of *The Didache*. The New Testament writers knew it was coming, and they often exhorted their fellow Christians to be glad, or at least hopeful, about it. Yet they recognized that the coming of the kingdom involved a stern test for every man who hoped to have a part in it, and that its coming would be associated with temptations and tribulations severe enough to give pause to the most confident.

"These last days" were days of grace in the simple untheological sense of a moratorium on the collection of a debt or the postponement of an examination. They were days in which people who had not prepared themselves for the coming trial were given an opportunity to make up for lost time. Rare indeed in the New Testament is the expression of a wish for the shortening of the moratorium.

These last days have extended for almost 2,000 years now out of the half-million or so in which man has inhabited the earth. They are numbered on our calendars and in our letters and official documents and books of account as days in the years of our Lord—*Anno Domini*. Occasionally somebody suggests that we should start numbering our years according to the atomic age or the space age, but the more perceptive among us realize that these great technical innovations do not come close to representing a crisis in human affairs comparable to the crisis that confronts every man in the fact of Jesus Christ.

In spite of the world-wide anxiety about the imminent possibility of a war that could destroy civilization, there is probably no real reason to think that the end of these years of grace is just around the corner today any more than it was in the days of Attila the Hun, the bubonic plague, or the barbarian invasion of Rome. Civilizations come and go, and the preaching of the Gospel remains.

And yet, the central theme of this durable Gospel is: "The end of all things is at hand." The kingdom of God is indeed just around the corner. Believe the good news and reorganize your life accordingly.

The question is not whether the day of judgment is coming tomorrow or next week, nor whether the atomic war will begin this year or next. It is not whether the Second Coming will occur in our lifetime or in that of our children. Rather, the question is what is temporary and what is permanent, what is subject to decay and what is eternal. The question is what kind of securities constitute the best investment for a prudent man, for "where your treasure is, there will your heart be also."

The Gospel—the Good News—is that God so loved the world that He gave His only begotten Son, that whosoever believeth in Him should not perish but have everlasting life. We of the laity, the *laos*, the people of God, have the privilege of so living and dying that our fellow men may see the hope that is in us and may look beyond us to the Saviour in whom we trust.

Grant, O Lord, that as we are baptized into the death of thy blessed Son, our Saviour Jesus Christ, so by continual mortifying our corrupt affections we may be buried with him; and that through the grave, and gate of death, we may pass to our joyful resurrection; for his merits, who died, and was buried, and rose again for us, the same thy Son Jesus Christ our Lord. Amen.

Book of Common Prayer, page 161